MEANS, ENDS,
AND
PERSONS

MEANS, ENDS,

AND

PERSONS

The Meaning and Psychological
Dimensions of Kant's Humanity Formula

Robert Audi

OXFORD
UNIVERSITY PRESS

Oxford University Press is a department of the University of Oxford. It furthers
the University's objective of excellence in research, scholarship, and education
by publishing worldwide. Oxford is a registered trade mark of Oxford University
Press in the UK and certain other countries.

Published in the United States of America by Oxford University Press
198 Madison Avenue, New York, NY 10016, United States of America.

Library of Congress Cataloging-in-Publication Data
Audi, Robert, Means, ends, and persons : The Meaning and Psychological
Dimensions of Kant's Humanity Formula / Robert Audi.
pages cm
Includes index.
ISBN 978-0-19-025155-0 (cloth); 978-0-19-091374-8 (paper)
1. Conduct of life. 2. Kant, Immanuel, 1724–1804. I. Title.
BJ1521.A93 2015170—dc23
2014046056

To Malou

CONTENTS

PREFACE

Ethics reaches beyond the hand and mouth, beyond our words and deeds, into the mind and heart. How good or bad we are is mainly a matter of our character, our intentions, and our patterns of treatment of others. All three of these go far beyond mere interpersonal behavior conceived as what we do with, to, and affecting one another. Novelists and poets have realized this multidimensionality of moral life, but moral philosophers have said too little about it. To be sure, the scope of ethics as portrayed in the virtue tradition is wide, and in Kant, a paradigmatic rule theorist in ethics, we find the famous humanity formula of his categorical imperative: we are to treat persons as ends and never merely as means. This is an intriguingly sweeping injunction. Almost everyone who reads Kant finds something that rings true in this directive, but its meaning, both within and outside Kant, is elusive. It is usually taken to indicate what actions we must avoid and, positively, what good deeds we should do for others. Whatever Kant's exact intention in stressing this directive, its scope is plausibly taken to be wide.

This book explores the scope of ethics and moral responsibility. It does this partly by clarifying the two kinds of treatment of persons that Kant and others have stressed—treatment of them merely as means and, by contrast, as ends. Kant's ethics has been an underlying inspiration for me, but (apart from a few pages in the text and a number of footnotes) the book will not be focused on Kant. Given that it does clarify the meaning of the concepts figuring centrally in the humanity formula, however, and also goes some distance toward justifying that principle—understood as I interpret it—the book may be viewed as contributing to understanding and supporting Kantian ethics broadly conceived. My aim is to introduce an *ethics of conduct*, to show how treatment of persons is a major instance of conduct, and, in doing this, to clarify the scope and standards of normative ethics.

Inevitably, normative questions will arise, and in framing them and suggesting a range of answers to some of them the book will contribute to the clarity and, in places, perhaps also the content of normative ethics. At various points, passages in Kant will be cited, and some of his views may be clarified by comparison and contrast with some of the ideas I present. But my chief purpose is to provide an account of the notion of conduct, and of treatment of persons in particular, that is a good resource for anyone interested in ethical theory, normative ethics, moral psychology, or the theory of action.

The book is written with the aim of intelligibility and usefulness for readers in four groups. One group is moral philosophers, moral psychologists, and other professionals working in ethics; another is students in any subfield of ethics; a third is readers of Kantian ethics; and the fourth comprises philosophers interested in the action-theoretic side of ethical theory—especially the nature of action, intention, motivation, and the behavioral manifestations of character. My aim is threefold: to develop a detailed account of the treatment of persons, to clarify the relation between the moral aspects of human behavior and its non-moral, descriptive aspects, and to explore the scope of the will and the corresponding range of our responsibilities for our conduct. Among the important implications of the book are these. On the theoretical side, ethics will emerge as an enterprise that must be more broadly conceived than is usual in the common frameworks of utilitarianism, rule theories (including Kant's), and even virtue ethics. This is a metaethical result. The book also has implications for normative ethics. It supports a wider conception of ethical behavior—roughly, of acting morally—than alternative views; it defends objectivity in moral appraisals of behavior; and it shows inadequacies in consent theories of moral justification.

The brevity of the book and its wealth of examples should make it readily understandable to students of ethics, including upper-level undergraduate students of philosophy. But there are also subtleties and various conceptual elements that should prove useful to professional readers. In some cases these are described; in others they are implicit in narrative examples or indicated in footnotes. Most of the footnotes are intended for readers with independent knowledge of the topic in question. The text is fully intelligible apart from the notes, but the points made in them may suggest further points or quite different examples. Throughout the book, the examples are intended both to illustrate a point being made and to be suggestive. I have often left much more to be said. I hope to have said enough to aid readers in discovering it.

ACKNOWLEDGMENTS

The topic of the treatment of persons and the distinction between treating them as means and as ends have been of great interest to me at least since the early 1980s. By the late 1990s, I had written in detail on these notions, and some of the basic ideas for this book were framed. The first formal presentation of some of those ideas may have been at the University of Glasgow in 2001, but some were also discussed in ethics seminars I directed much earlier with my then colleague, Stephen Kalish. Since those occasions I have benefited from presentations I have given at Australian Catholic University, Georgetown University, the Greater Pittsburgh Area Philosophical Society, the Iowa Philosophical Society, the Jaggielonian University, Macalaster College, the Rocky Mountain Ethics Congress, the United States Military Academy (at West Point), and the Universities of Arkansas (Little Rock), California, Riverside, Cardiff, Notre Dame, Rome (III), the Redlands, Santa Clara, and Texas (Austin). More colleagues and students than I can recall have been of great help in developing this book. I would particularly like to thank Karl Ameriks, Paul Audi, Carla Bagnoli, Dustin Crummett, John Deigh, Brad Hooker, Jimmy Lenman, Alasdair MacIntyre, Hugh McCann, Onora O'Neill, Jack Sammons, the late Robert Solomon, Jens Timmermann, Mark Timmons, Peter Wicks, anonymous readers, and, especially, Roger Crisp and Derek Parfit, both of whom provided insightful comments on a full early draft.

I have also benefited greatly from a fellowship in the Notre Dame Institute for Advanced Study during the fall of 2013, where John Haldane, Lynn Joy, and Jean Porter raised helpful points, and from assistance from the Press. My editor, Peter Ohlin, has provided advice and help at several stages in the development of the final text, and I have benefited from indexing and proofreading by Daniel Immerman, from copyediting by Ginny Faber, from Emily Sacharin's help with jacket and copy design, and from Mary Jo Rhodes' skillful guidance of the production process.

MEANS, ENDS,

AND

PERSONS

INTRODUCTION

Human action is shot through with instrumentality. We regularly use things as means to accomplish something, and we often treat others as our means to achieve what we cannot achieve on our own. But are persons ever instruments, or, if they are, ever properly so? And may we ever justifiably treat persons as means? These questions are closely connected with two that, historically, ethics has taken as normatively central: What should we do? and What kinds of persons should we be? The first concerns the actions we ought to perform and is widely considered the central question for rule ethics; the second concerns the traits of character we ought to have and is widely considered central for virtue ethics.

No plausible ethical theory denies the importance of either question, but there is a third question about the scope of ethics that has not been generally distinguished from these two and is both important in itself and a pathway to understanding the relation between moral action and moral character. I propose to call this the *conduct question*. It is the question of what kinds of conduct we should engage in, where conduct is three-dimensional: not simply action, but—in ways to be described—the performance of an action *of* a certain type, *for* a certain reason, and *in* a certain way. Clear cases of conduct are treating persons as ends and treating them merely as means. Think of a mother lovingly changing her baby or, by contrast, of someone who, asking for a loan in a sincere-sounding way, lies to you in order to defraud you. The former illustrates conduct good in all three dimensions: act-type (as changing the baby), motivation (maternal love), and manner (being lovingly done). The latter is immoral in all three: act-type (as lying), motivation (as exploitive), and manner (as hypocritically performed, manifesting a suspiciously golden touch that is at odds with the agent's intention). The affectionate maternal conduct illustrates treatment as an end; the manipulative conduct is a case of objectionably treating someone as a means—quite likely *merely* so, in a sense to be clarified.

The notion of treating persons as ends in themselves— call it *end-regarding treatment*—and, by contrast, the notion of treating them merely as means—call it *merely instrumental treatment*—are best known through Kantian ethics; but both notions, or at least closely similar ones, have independent uses in moral discourse. Both types of conduct, moreover, are often cited in ethical literature as support for moral judgments. Treating someone merely as a means merits disapproval, and treating people as ends merits approval and is to be encouraged. Both notions can (and I think should) be grounded and clarified outside Kant's writings, as well as explicated in a way that reveals how Kant apparently understood them. In providing an account of these two notions, this book will clarify the ethical importance of the conduct question—the question of what kinds of conduct we should engage in. In doing that it also provides a basis for understanding Kantian ethics so that it can take account of character, motivation, and certain elements of behavior in a way that it cannot if, as is common, it is conceived as a deontological rule theory standing in stark contrast with virtue ethics.

The possibility of understanding merely instrumental and end-regarding treatment of persons without reliance on Kant leaves open the related question whether they can also be characterized without reliance on moral notions. That question is important both for ethical theory in general and for clarifying Kantian ethics. For suppose that understanding whether someone is treating another person merely as a means presupposes moral appraisals, say that the first is wronging the second; and, on the positive side, suppose that understanding whether one person is treating another as an end also presupposes moral appraisals, for instance that the first is respecting the moral rights of the second. Then the injunctions to promote the latter treatment and avoid the former will be understandable only if the presupposed moral appraisals are. The appeal to these two injunctions as standards of conduct or in support of moral judgments would be understandable only on the basis of *prior* understanding of the presupposed moral judgments and, equally important, justified only on the basis of independent ground for them. If, for instance, we have to know that one person *wronged* or violated the *rights* of another in order to know that the first treated the second merely as a means, then merely instrumental treatment cannot be taken to be morally objectionable on its own account.

If, by contrast, the two standards of treatment are (as I shall argue) explicable without appeal to moral concepts, then these standards can also serve, in ways to be described, as important anchors of moral judgment—descriptive, "factual" anchors that can warrant positive and negative moral appraisals. They can yield a way of seeing what we ought and ought not to do, rather than just an evaluative description of conduct that reflects some *other* basis of moral appraisal, whether Kantian, utilitarian, intuitionist, or of some other kind. An account of these standards of treatment of persons, then, can enhance our understanding of both Kantian and other ethical theories.

In developing an account of an ethics of conduct, the book proceeds by bringing resources from action theory and moral psychology to bear on understanding both treating

persons as ends and treating them merely as means. Each
kind of treatment represents conduct, in a sense of this term
that the book explains. It explicates the notions of merely
instrumental and end-regarding treatment independently of
Kant, but it does so in a way that both helps in understanding
some of his main ideas and enhances the usefulness of the
two notions in ethics.

Among the broadest major views for which I argue are
these. First, treating someone merely as a means can be explicated in a non-valuational—roughly, "descriptive"—way.
Second, treating someone as an end can be explicated without appeal to *moral* concepts, even if not independently of
valuational notions, such as the notion of what is good for a
person. Third, treatment of either kind is multidimensional.
As conduct, it involves not only more than action alone but
also more than action viewed in relation to its motivation,
and this implies that our responsibility for our conduct goes
far beyond our strictly behavioral obligations: obligations to
do the right deeds.

I have already indicated why it is important to achieve
an explication of the notions of merely instrumental and
end-regarding treatment of persons that does not rely on
moral concepts, but let me add this. Normative properties, of which moral properties are paradigms, are not
brute. Take an epistemological analogy. Just as beliefs are
justified, or unjustified, on the basis of other properties,
say being memory-based or having the believed content
visually represented, acts are right, wrong, or obligatory
on the basis of other properties, such as being promised
or, on the negative side, deadly. No act is brutely right,
wrong, or obligatory, as no belief is brutely justified or
unjustified. Things possess normative properties in virtue of—*consequentially upon*—possessing other properties: those constituting the *base* of the former. These base
properties, moreover, may be considered *descriptive* in

a sense implying (among other things) that to attribute them to something (say a person or action) is to characterize them in a way that plays a role in individuating them, singling them out as distinct from other things; it is not to ascribe either intrinsic value or disvalue or a deontic property such as obligation.

The consequentiality of normative properties on descriptive ones entails what is called the strong supervenience of the former on the latter, but it implies more. Suppose, for instance, that (as supervenience requires) two actions that do not differ in their descriptive non-normative properties cannot differ in their normative properties either, say one being right and the other wrong.[1] Suppose I were perfectly duplicated in psychological and other natural properties. My duplicate, who would have (perhaps with exceptions not relevant here) the same intentions, beliefs, and character traits, would be exactly as good. It does not follow from this supposition alone that normative properties are consequential on non-normative ones, or even grounded on them in any other way, for instance causally. But, as I will illustrate in many ways, they surely are consequential properties.

Not only are moral properties consequential on non-normative ones, but plainly, in life as we know it our *knowledge* of the former is based on knowledge, or at least

---

1. This needs qualifications not important here; e.g., two act-tokens even with the same agent will differ in some temporal property, and even a perfect duplicate would differ at least in some spatial property. There is also an abstract possibility of a kind of basic moral knowledge an omnipotent being might simply implant in someone, without the person's having any grounds. For a detailed study of supervenience see Karen Bennett and Brian McLaughlin, "Supervenience," *Stanford Encyclopedia* (2005) http://plato.stanford.edu.entries/supervenience/, 1–42.

on grounds for knowledge, of the latter. If, for instance, I know someone has good character, it will be on the basis of knowledge of some of the person's intentions and beliefs; and, typically, if I know nothing about these, I lack knowledge of the person's character.[2] This is crucial for understanding treatment of persons and other normative notions. Given the epistemic—roughly evidential—dependence of these notions on descriptive notions, we need to know how to ascertain their applicability without relying on other moral notions if we are to use the treatment notions in doing basic work in the ethical appraisal of persons and their conduct.

Part I (chapters 1–4) explains what constitutes merely instrumental treatment and shows how knowledge of it is possible. Its grounding in, and knowability through, descriptive, often perceptible, properties is important because it enables us to achieve a kind of objectivity in moral appraisal. We may unmistakably see one person stealthily remove a woman's wallet from her handbag; this provides an objective basis for a judgment of wrongdoing. Given the ready inferability of the presence of certain normative properties from

2. For explanation and defense of this perhaps only moderately controversial claim, see my "Ethical Naturalism and the Explanatory Power of Moral Concepts," in Steven Wagner and Richard Warner, eds., *Naturalism: A Critical Appraisal* (Notre Dame, IN: University of Notre Dame Press, 1993), 95–115, and *Moral Perception* (Princeton, NJ: Princeton University Press, 2013). Much pertinent discussion and many references bearing on the topic are found in Aaron Zimmerman's *Moral Epistemology* (New York: Routledge, 2010). I should add that the point in the text is not restricted to firsthand knowledge because we can know from reliable *testimony* (hence not have firsthand knowledge) that someone is, say, morally good without knowing anything specific about the person's intentions or beliefs.

the presence of their grounds, we can achieve such objectivity largely though using common-sense observations of the grounding properties.[3] The kinds of grounds in question will be illustrated in many places in this book.

None of this implies that there is no case for skepticism about the possibility of the relevant kind of non-normative, "descriptive" knowledge, say about whether a statement is a lie or an action injures someone. But, whether the cognitions in question constitute knowledge or simply justified belief, there is surely good reason for trusting many of them as a basis of rational moral judgments. Such descriptive cognition *is* widely trusted in any case, and its status in grounding moral and other normative knowledge should be kept in mind. It will be illustrated by many of my examples, most of which suggest that we in fact can know or at least justifiedly believe that a person has treated others merely as means or failed to treat them as ends.

Part II (chapters 4–6) explicates the notion of treating persons as ends in themselves (I will often omit 'in themselves', but it is presupposed in the kinds of contexts that concern me). In doing this, the book will reveal much about how the value of persons is to be conceived and what it means to act for their sake in the way morality often requires of us. The two parts of the book correspond to two—perhaps the central two—concerns of ethics as a guide to interpersonal life: preventing harm and enhancing well-being, where in

---

3. I presuppose the notion of a perceptible "descriptive" property, but a theory of such properties is presented in my *Moral Perception* (Princeton, NJ: Princeton University Press, 2013). There I argue that genuine moral perception is possible; but, for reasons that will become apparent in this book, conduct as instanced by merely instrumental and end-regarding treatment is of a kind and complexity that make it uncertain whether it is ever perceptible in the sense in which, say, overt wrongdoing may be.

both cases this guiding role concerns ways that manifest or at least accord with respect for others *as persons*.[4] If Part I articulates a perspective on how certain kinds of conduct toward persons—even some that appears beneficent—is wrongful and may be prevented by conscientious moral agents, Part II provides a conception of how our conduct toward persons should manifest respect for them.

Beyond providing a general account of instrumental and end-regarding treatment, I undertake other tasks that have not so far been accomplished. I show the importance of the distinction between *solely* and *merely* instrumental treatment, and I distinguish *treatment* of persons—as a paradigm of conduct toward them—from action that simply *affects* them, which may be casual and may not be morally significant. It also clarifies the scope of intention, the range of commands and resolutions, the dimensions of moral responsibility, and the distinction between end-regarding and rights-respecting treatment. In doing all this, the book both enriches and refines the vocabulary of moral appraisal. As teachers of Kantian ethics know, too often the injunction to avoid treating people merely as means is taken too broadly, as prohibiting treatment of them as means *at all*. But treating others as means in certain ways is inevitable in normal human relations, and we need a way of describing the conditions under which it is unobjectionable. What is needed in this and similar cases of conduct, and is developed in this book, is an account of the kinds of instrumental treatment of persons that are wrong and the kinds that are permissible. Permissible

4. For discussion of various kinds of respect that should be considered in understanding this point, see Stephen E. Darwall, *The Second-Person Standpoint: Respect, Morality, and Accountability* (Cambridge, MA: Harvard University Press, 2006). His "recognition respect," which is implicit in human dignity as often conceived, seems primary here.

conduct, to be sure, need not be praiseworthy. Morality tolerates far more than it applauds. Even end-regarding treatment may not rise to the level of laudability. Moral appraisal is highly discriminating. This book shows why that is so and explains in part how an understanding of that fact can be a positive element in reinforcing interpersonal conduct.

PART I

THE ETHICS OF PROTECTING PERSONS

1

THE INSTRUMENTAL TREATMENT
OF PERSONS

Nearly everyone has had the unpleasant sense of being "used." Consider being invited to a dinner party only to discover that it is purely the information one can give the host, and not one's company, that is wanted, with the result that after a short conversation one is largely ignored. Or think of being visited by an acquaintance at an inconvenient time when, one later learns, the person needed an alibi. 'You used me' is a natural complaint in such cases, and it commonly indicates conduct at least approaching treating someone merely as a means. Here one may be reminded of Kant's *Groundwork*, though the idea is, as we shall see, intelligible and morally important in its own right. Still, the notions of treating persons merely as means and, by contrast, as ends are so closely associated with Kant that an account that is independent of him should begin with some of their ordinary moorings. Consider first the general notion of using things as means.

I. Means and Ends

Using things as means is pervasive. Commonly, it is employing one thing in order to achieve an end. Actions themselves can also be means, and they can be instrumental even if they do not succeed. Such instrumental deeds are doing something with a view to bringing about a result. One can spray poison ivy as a means (or at least an attempted means) of eliminating it even if one fails to do this and succeeds only in *trying* to do it. Instruments are paradigms of means, though even persons can also be means. We understand quite well what it is to use something as an instrument, and I begin by clarifying the notion of instrumental action.

Instrumental actions are those performed in order to realize a further end, as opposed to those that are performed "for their own sake" and, in that sense, *intrinsically motivated*. Instrumental actions must be understood relationally, as in a way subordinate to the ends to which they are means; their "point" lies beyond them, in various ways that will soon be evident. Acting instrumentally is a kind of action pervasive in normal lives, and I take the end aimed at in so acting to be a state of affairs, an event, or an action. Understanding the distinction between instrumental and intrinsically motivated actions can be difficult because one can do a single thing *both* for an instrumental reason and for its own sake. On a free evening, aware that one needs exercise but wanting to enjoy the soft light and gentle breeze, one could walk in a meadow both in order to exercise and just for its intrinsic attractiveness, as where one walks simply for pleasure. Each reason could indeed be sufficient: one would (other things being equal) take the walk on either count alone. People may differ in how often they act for two different, individually sufficient reasons, but the possibility is easy to understand and often realized. As this case indicates, actions can be instrumental quite apart from whether objects, such as a machete designed to clear bushes blocking one's path, are used as means in the process.

To use something as a means, then (in the common, instrumental way that is in question), is to employ it to bring about an end that, in at least two respects, is distinct from the means. First, the end is conceptually distinct: the concept of the end does not essentially contain that of the means in question. This is illustrated where one's end is opening a stuck window and one's means is a paint scraper. The end might be conceived in the same way if, instead, the intended means were a screwdriver. The point also holds for actions as ends. Suppose my end is to collect information about a foreign country. Neither the concept of my means, which might be a more knowledgeable friend I consult for information, nor any particular concept of my friend even when the friend is my means, figures essentially in my concept of the end. The second point is that ends as such are instrumentally open: in principle they can be realized by more than one means (I am speaking only of ends that *can* be realized).[1] Collecting information, for instance, is an end in which the friend need not figure at all; one could use a guidebook. In each example, there is both the thing constituting a means, the "instrument," such as the scraper or the book, and the instrumental action of using it, such as consulting the book. It will help to explore other kinds of example, and here I will focus on instrumental treatment, which I take to entail a kind of instrumental use of some person or thing.

Consider first a case of purely instrumental treatment of something: using something *solely* as a means. Such action implies at least this: that the thing is used *only* in order to bring about an end conceptually distinct from it. By contrast, think of playing a piano not (for instance) to relax, but for its own sake: as an end in itself. This activity has, as its goal,

---

1. Granted, one's end could be *action-specific,* say to wake someone by playing a resounding chord opening a certain Beethoven sonata. But there are many ways to do even this: a specific action's figuring in the end does not foreclose a plurality of ways to achieve it.

playing *it* (rewardingly); the agent is not playing it to bring about something in which playing is not conceptually (and in fact) essential.[2] Consider also pursuing, as an end, composing music, which is possible in thought alone. This is to pursue it for its own sake: on account of qualities one takes to be intrinsic to it, not for what it causes.

Composing music and walking in a meadow are things an agent brings about. Persons, however, are not the sorts of things that are brought about, and this raises the question of what it is to treat them as, indeed even to *have* them as, ends (in themselves). This question will be pursued in detail in Part II, but a preliminary discussion is needed here to clarify the notion of treating as a means by contrast with that of treating as an end. Reference to non-actions as ends of conduct is common and at least as ancient as Aristotle.[3] Thus, one might say, "Money is not an end in itself." The notion of treating a person, or even a "thing," as an end seems, moreover, to be explicable in terms of the concept of a state of affairs, an action, or an event, as an end—hence in terms of things that can be brought about. We do not need a new concept of an end to explicate such treatment.

2. One can do something to bring about pleasure instrumentally; but (e.g.) playing an instrument in order to *cause* pleasure in oneself is not doing it *for* pleasure.

3. In the *Nicomachean Ethics*, 1094a5-10, e.g., Aristotle says the ends we seek "appear to differ; some are activities, and others are products of the activities," and (later) indicates the diversity of ends: "Since there are many actions, crafts, and sciences, the ends turn out to be many as well; for health is the end of medicine, a boat of boatbuilding, victory of generalship ..." (Terence Irwin, trans. [Indianapolis: Hackett, 1999]). Granted, the notion of treating persons as ends may have originated with Kant; nevertheless, there are underlying analogies—and many uses of language—that enable us to explicate the notion independently of him.

To see what constitutes treating things (including persons) as ends, consider how some people treat a painting as an end rather than, say, as an investment. There must simply be something suitably connected with the end that one pursues for its own sake, say *viewing* the painting. We may also refer to other substances and to such things as a beautiful garden as our ends; but this notion of an end ("in itself") should be understood in terms of bringing about some state of affairs, event, or action, in which the thing in question figures. If my end is a beautiful garden, I will tend to seek means to producing one. Talk of treating persons as ends—at least in ethical contexts—is explicable in terms of action in which persons figure in intrinsically motivated (end-regarding) action.

None of this implies that there is no general notion of a person *as an end*, in a normative sense, say as a being with the distinctive kind of value that goes with human dignity and for the sake of which we should act in certain ways. This notion of dignity or some similar notion may indeed help to explain why persons *should* be treated as ends. The point here is that treating persons (indeed other entities as well) as ends does not require a new basic category of motivated action.

II. Instrumental versus End-Regarding Treatment

The core idea in instrumental treatment, then, is that of using its object not as something valued in itself (even if it happens to be so valued) but to achieve a *further* end. The core idea in treatment of something *as an end* is roughly that of acting in order to bring about something in which the object is essential and figures non-instrumentally and non-contingently. The main contrast is this: Whereas the importance, for the agent's aim(s) in acting, of what is treated only as a means is contingent—since in principle the agent might believe another means will serve—the importance, for the agent, of what is treated as an end is essential for the aim(s) in acting.[4] If I am walking in the meadow just to get exercise, then I will cease wanting to do it if I come to believe that it will not yield exercise. I will also tend to prefer another means to getting exercise if I think of a comparably convenient one that I consider better. If something is wanted *just* instrumentally, then, the agent will tend to put it aside or abandon it upon coming to believe that something else would be a better way to achieve the end in question.

Suppose, by contrast, that I am walking in the meadow wholly for its own sake; then my interest is in the character of the activity itself. I will be *open* to influence by what I discover about how to achieve the kind of walk I want or about its effects. I would, for instance, turn back if I discovered I was damaging newly planted grass. But doing or bringing about anything I do not see as intrinsic to the walk is not a reason why I am walking.

Several further points will add clarity here. First, a means to something unimportant can itself be important, whether derivatively or even inherently (thus "in itself"). Second, instrumental means as usually understood—the kind in question in this book—contrast with what are sometimes called *constitutive means*. A means is constitutive when it partly constitutes, and so is essential to, the end, as playing

4. No one would ordinarily speak of treating a person as an end where the agent aims at causing pain in the person for its own sake, but this could be non-instrumental treatment. For theoretical completeness, then, we could speak of positive and negative treatment of persons as ends. This book implicitly clarifies the latter, but there is no need to consider it further, and I will use 'end-regarding' only where the end the agent aims at is of a positive kind.

the cello is essential to the pleasure of doing so. The playing is a means because it is done *for* pleasure and is one's way of achieving it; the playing is constitutive of one's end because the *kind* of pleasure in question is sought *in* the playing. Third, the playing does not by itself *wholly* constitute the end because it can fail to yield the pleasure. Success is also contingent in the instrumental cases that concern us: instrumental treatment of something as a means to an end does not imply success in achieving that end.

These points suggest a fourth. The relevant instrumental relations—those determining whether one person's treatment of another is instrumental—include those the agent *takes* to hold, whether they do hold or not. Thus, from the point of view of determining whether, on some occasion, we are treating people merely as means, what we then *believe* about our actions toward them is a central element.[5] Suppose that in seeking to gain something for ourselves, we believe Sue will serve as a means of getting it despite risks to herself. This belief may suffice to satisfy the cognitive condition for treating her merely as a means in the activity of persuading her to try for it, say finding a lost cellphone in a dangerous neighborhood, even if this belief is mistaken and she will refuse and so not serve as a means. We can be treated *as* a means without actually *being* a means. Treating someone so does not imply the occurrence of the end, and one cannot be an actual means to what does not occur. As this indicates, we can also be treated *merely* as a means without being a means (since the end is not achieved) and, secondly, if the end is

5. The notion does not preclude failing to believe the person so treated *is* a person. Stretching to reach a high shelf in a dark room, a careless searcher might stand on an unconscious person taken to be a sand-filled cushion. This kind of case need not concern us.

somehow achieved by the agent, without being a means to that end at all. Someone could manipulatively lie to you to get your money by offering high interest for a fraudulent loan but, instead, get the money because a confederate, noticing the failed attempt to defraud you, steals it.

So far, we have seen much about instrumental treatment but have left implicit what counts as treatment of a person in the first place. This is a difficult question and not generally explored in depth in ethical literature that deals with merely instrumental or end-regarding treatment. Seven points will help here. Some are negative, and I begin with two of those.

First, although much action toward one or more others is treatment, not all of it is: a momentary "automatic" smile at a person one quickly passes on a campus is a (single-agent) social action, but not a kind of treatment of the person. Brevity is not the reason, however: crowding a person off a sidewalk could be equally momentary but would be a case of bad treatment. These examples show the second point: that treatment need not be intentional. The smiling and crowding, for instance, may or may not be intentional. Another example is treating people guardedly. This could be part of someone's way of, say, relating to new acquaintances. It may or may not be intentional, as where soft voice is unintentionally used in first meetings.

Third, not all action affecting others is treatment: my momentary smile may cause a similar response in another person; but this alone does not entail that it constitutes a kind of treatment. Catching my shoe on a paving block could also evoke a smile. It is clearly not treatment of the person it amuses. Fourth, although it might seem that treatment must always affect one or more others, this is not so—at least on the plausible assumption that spying on others (which need not affect them) is a way of treating them. (Such cases will be discussed in chapter 7.) We should not conclude, however—and this is my fifth point—that treatment must be social: there are surely good and bad ways to treat oneself, and some will be illustrated in later chapters.

More positively, and my sixth point: treatment of someone is, in the most typical cases, morally significant action toward the person. But it need not be. Treating a passerby as an information source in getting directions need not be morally significant. This case does suggest a positive element, however (and this is my seventh point): treatment of a person is a way of acting that is morally responsible in the sense that (whether blameworthy or not) it may be appropriately assessed in moral terms. This of course holds of at least most social actions, including even such unintentional ones as treating an unconscious person as a seat on a dark, crowded train. But not all social actions imply treatment.

None of this provides a definition of what constitutes treatment of persons—unless the idea of acting *toward* a person is conceived as a very rough one. But given these points and the accounts to be offered for merely instrumental and end-regarding treatment—the most important kinds—uncertainties about the boundaries of the generic notion of treatment will not undermine the overall position of this book. With this background, I want first to sketch an account of the notion of treating a person *merely* as a means. Once that is before us, we can better understand treating persons as ends.

III. Treating Solely as a Means versus Merely as a Means

We might begin with a distinction commonly overlooked and rarely examined. It might seem that we should conceive treating something or some person merely as a means to some end, *E,* as using the thing or person to bring about *E* and *only* for that purpose. This is not so; 'merely' usually has a derogatory element we must capture, as with calling a point 'merely terminological' or a change in a document 'merely cosmetic'. Suppose I invite Tim (an acquaintance) to join me on a walk, *only* to avoid being found alone by my angry cousin: I have no interest in Tim's serving as a means to any other end or in his good. In walking with him, then, I am not treating him as an end. Perhaps I *should* be treating him as an end, since that is appropriate to such friendly social activities; but that does not always occur in human relations of this kind. Nonetheless, it certainly does not follow that I am treating him merely as a means.

To see this, notice that my friendly relation to Tim and my present motivational character—notwithstanding the instrumental reason for which I am now acting—are such that if I learned that he felt ill, I would (even with no new basic desires) become concerned and would reverse course to get him home. By contrast, if I were sufficiently callous—say the kind of person who insensitively uses others to accomplish my aims—I would proceed utterly irrespective of Tim's discomfort or anything else not relevant to my aim in walking with him. This would be the kind of thing that indicates treating him *merely* as a means; for I would be concerned only with Tim's instrumental function in separating me from my cousin *and* would (in a way to be clarified below) be disposed not to respond to any aspects or foreseeable changes of my conduct, such as reducing his discomfort, that are not instrumentally relevant to achieving my end.

The crucial distinction the case illustrates is between treating *solely* (*only*) *as a means* and treating *merely as a means*. The former does not entail the latter. For the latter, the instrumental function of the action in question, or some set of instrumental functions, must be in a certain way one's *exclusive* aim.[6] An instrumental aim governing treatment of

6. I assume that the action is intentional under the relevant description and that in *A-ing* intentionally *S* (an agent) treats *x* as

someone is exclusive, in the relevant sense, only if it rules out certain kinds of opposing motives. Thus, if I were treating Tim merely, hence exclusively, as a means to keeping me from being found alone, then—given no change in my motivational character at the time—his discomfort might not (and likely would not) even partly motivate me to help him unless I took it to bear on this aim, say because it might make him cough and thus reveal my whereabouts.[7]

Compare this case with one in which I ask directions of a passerby. I treat such people only as means where I treat them solely as information sources. I might *believe* they are much more than this, but the character of my treatment may be unaffected by such positive background beliefs about their value. Still, even if getting directions is my *only* purpose, my desires in the situation are normally such that I would help a passerby who, after giving me directions, started to choke on a snack, whereas someone who was treating the person *merely* as a means and had gotten the directions before the choking started would tend to walk on. Granted, a new motive, such as impressing bystanders with my first-aid skills, could arise in the latter case and indeed prevail. Possible new motives are not in question here but will be considered shortly.

The kind of difference exhibited by the contrasting versions of the example requesting information of a passerby illustrates what I call the *solely-merely contrast*. Treating merely as a means should be understood in a way that coheres with the appropriateness of 'mere' in 'treating as a

a means to *E*, the end the agent seeks. This is possible even if *E* is not achieved. By contrast, *A-ing* can *be* a means to *E* without being intentional or even performed knowingly. Burning grass can be a means by which I kill mosquitoes, even if I burn it unknowingly.

7. Whether the discomfort would in fact motivate me largely depends on the constraints built into my psychology. Such constraints are discussed below.

mere means' when disapprovingly applied to interpersonal conduct. Treating *as a mere means*, however, in the usual sense implying abuse or shabby or depreciatory treatment, is not equivalent to treating merely as a means (as examples below will make clear); but the latter may well instantiate those or similar kinds of bad treatment. The implication of 'treating someone *as a mere means*' is that the person, even if not conceived by the agent as unimportant, is, in or during the treatment, at least not valued by the agent as more than a means.[8] This implication need not hold for treating someone merely as a means. The modifier 'merely as a means' concerns the manner and motivation of the action; 'as a mere means' typically concerns the *object* of the action—or at least the agent's attitude toward the object. Treating merely as a means is possible (if quite unlikely) even regarding people the agent values, in an overall way, non-instrumentally and even highly.

A natural assumption about how to determine proper treatment is that the manner in which a thing should be treated is at least largely determined by what the thing is. Reflection on examples of the kind we have already considered—and indeed, reflection on some of the major ethical theories, such as Aristotle's and Kant's—shows that persons are never plausibly considered mere means. One might think that *nothing* of value is properly viewed thus. But consider a foul-tasting pill that I am given by my host for indigestion and lose on the lawn. One natural response might be: Don't worry about it; it's just a means

---

8. The proposed view may suggest that morally decent people rarely treat others merely as means. I hope so, but I take no position on this empirical question. My aim is to clarify the concept (perhaps with a degree of rational reconstruction consistent with its intuitive functioning).

(or merely a means) to temporary relief and we have plenty of them. Here the response does not imply that the pill has no value.

In any case, persons never *are* mere means. Can a person ever be a means at all? One might think not—on the ground that even if persons can be treated as means, they can never *be* that. But surely teachers commonly want to be and may in fact be means to students' learning a subject. This may also be said hypothetically, as when teachers have just finished the requisite training and done no teaching because no student has yet appeared for tutelage.

The two kinds of "negative" instrumental treatment we have been comparing have something in common. Both in treating someone merely as a means and in treating someone as a mere means, the agent, in acting, is *unconcerned* with anything about the person so treated that is not relevant to realizing the agent's end.[9] But, at least in the case of treating merely as a means, the agent is both intent on getting the end *and* disposed *not* to form any independent non-instrumental desire toward the other person, say wanting, for its own sake,

---

9. An alternative formulation would preface the point with 'other things equal', since the action could be affected by some other end in relation to which the agent is not treating the person merely instrumentally. A captain might treat a junior officer merely as a means to guiding them to a shelter, but also value the subordinate as an end qua good tennis partner, hence be unwilling to put the officer at high risk. We might then say the subordinate would be treated merely as a means to shelter *insofar* as that does not interfere with serving the other end. The same complexity seems better accommodated, however, by the discussion (below) of motivation and constraints. But if an action is performed so as to yield treating someone merely as a means, intrinsic concern with the person's good is still ruled out as *motivating* the action.

to make the person comfortable.[10] This disposition is not required for treating someone solely (only) as a means. Its presence in *merely* instrumental treatment largely explains why the instrumental analogy is so apt: instruments (as such) are disposable once their purpose is achieved.

Much could be said about what constitutes a disposition of the relevant kind. Two points may help to locate the relevant notion. First, I am assuming that what a person is disposed to do—and I include acts of omission—is such that, on the supposition that the disposition is present, the person's doing it does not in general stand in need of explanation. Second, under certain conditions, i.e., conditions favorable to the manifestation of the disposition (in ways illustrated in our examples), the person's *not* doing it *does* stand in need of explanation. Third, where the disposition is to do certain deeds or to act in a certain way, the deeds or ways of acting, if they are manifestations of the disposition (which they need not always be) will be explainable by appeal to something in the "nature" of the agent, at least in terms of the agent's motivation at the time, but sometimes also in terms of a trait of character or enduring aim, project, or other volitional element.

Good instruments, of course, are usually such that they can serve many purposes, and we may care much about an instrument on that count. But this is not caring about the instrument for its own sake, say as one might about an elegant carving knife. An office manager who encourages and

10. To be sure, since one could treat someone merely as a means to two or more ends, one end could constrain another: the agent could be disposed to form a desire to treat the person better in relation to realizing the first end *on account of* the positive role that realizing it plays in achieving the second. Still, the agent is disposed not to be motivated by any *non*-instrumental consideration. Mixed motivation is accounted for in other ways below.

protects the best typist need not be treating the typist as an end. Treating someone in a given way for a *further* end, even if the end is consistent with the person's well-being, is not treating the person *as* an end.

The treatment of persons is a central focus of morality. Any plausible moral theory must provide standards governing it even if the terminology of means and ends does not play a major role in the theory. But much would be lost by any comprehensive ethics in which those notions are not employed to good purpose. Human actions are incomprehensible apart from some actual or possible end at which they are aimed; and action aimed at an end beyond it—which is by far the most common case—is performed at least partly as a means. Persons may be a means by which we achieve an end, but they are never mere means. Even treatment of someone solely as a means does not imply viewing the person as mere means or treating that person merely as such. We have seen some of the reasons that the latter, merely instrumental treatment is objectionable. Much more must be said about why it is objectionable and, given that it is, how it can be avoided.

2

INSTRUMENTAL TREATMENT
AS HUMAN CONDUCT

Ethical theory has often been concerned with the moral status of actions conceived as momentary. Much of what we do, however, is extended in time. This particularly applies to treatment of persons, which often occurs over a long period. To be sure, momentary actions may be partly constitutive of treatment; and treatment over time, as with parents' behavior in relation to their children, may be constituted by related instances of conduct each of which is quite short. In any of these cases, we may have a high degree of control over how we treat someone. Here the ethics of treatment must address the kind and degree of our moral responsibility for our conduct.

I. The Motivation and Controllability
of Merely Instrumental Conduct

Instrumental motivation can be strong. We can care much about what we use only or even merely as an instrument. Moreover, something used merely as an instrument can *become* important in its own right. Human motivation is highly sensitive to circumstances. Thus, an agent's being unconcerned with the non-instrumental aspects of an instrument—or the non-instrumental significance of a person being treated merely as a means—does not entail being incapable of *acquiring* a caring concern. That concern may be acquired either during the time the conduct occurs or later. Some people who would take no account of a coughing fit in someone they are treating merely as a means *would* assist that person with an apparent heart attack.

To see how conduct may change in midstream, suppose that in the course of my treating Tim merely as a means to avoiding my angry cousin, he coughs with sounds like those of my father's highly distinctive coughing. A new element may arise: a sentimental sympathy I usually lack. This element need not stem from my moral character or, as we might assume with the heart attack, from some potentially opposing motive I already have, such as a standing desire, activated in the context, to help people in medical emergencies.

Both cases of possible changes in merely instrumental treatment show that although treating someone merely as a means is not in fact accompanied by non-instrumental motivation toward the person—a negative point clearly entailed by the use of 'merely'—merely instrumental treatment can nevertheless be altered by the formation of such motivation. Given a certain foresightful self-interest, a sudden realization of how a person one is manipulating and treating merely as a means can assist one could produce a desire, even a somewhat beneficent desire, to be supportive. This may greatly alter and perhaps improve the treatment. The treatment may still, however, be merely instrumental. Think of a callous prison guard who is treating a prisoner merely as a means to getting information about co-conspirators. Realizing that the prisoner can sing and tell stories might mitigate the harshness of the guard's manipulative treatment. Over time, it might even evoke a liking for the prisoner, and that liking could eliminate the merely instrumental treatment.

Engaging in merely instrumental treatment, then, need not make one impervious to new motives that produce concern for others and alter both the motivation and the manner of the treatment. Merely instrumental treatment need not be either *unalterable* or *irreversible*. It does not preclude the formation either of new, mitigating influences or of overriding motivation. These points apply particularly where treatment is (as is common) extended in time, say in leading someone through a forest. Where 'treat' has a continuous present sense, for instance when we speak of how parents treat their child, the reference is usually to temporally extended conduct.

Part of the contrast between reversible and irreversible instrumental treatment is expressible in possible worlds terminology. In the case of walking with Tim in the normal way in which I treat him solely, but not merely, as a means, there are nearby worlds (roughly, similar situations) in which I reverse course and cease my instrumental treatment, then begin treating him as an end. If, by contrast, I am treating him merely as a means, the reversal worlds are further away. They may be very far off if my callousness is mitigable only by an unlikely causal factor, such as a cough's resembling my father's.

Treating someone solely as a means, then, may again be seen as quite different from treating a person merely so. If I am a morally decent person, then where I treat Tim solely, but not merely, as a means (1) I will *not* be disposed not to be influenced by non-instrumental concerns, which leaves open that a reversal world is nearby, as where I would reverse course if he merely ceased wanting to walk; and (2) I will have the normal friendly desires which, though not motivating my behavior at the time, are easily manifested when his discomfort or coughing make them relevant. These friendly desires—especially the kind that go with *empathy*—bring reversal worlds closer than they are for a callous person. Merely instrumental treatment entails solely instrumental treatment, but the converse does not hold. Moreover, solely instrumental treatment in simple routine conduct, especially toward people one does not know, seems common.

II. Constraints, Moral Character, and Self-Control

Merely instrumental treatment of persons, I have maintained, need not be irreversible. Readiness for reversibility, moreover, comes in degrees and, in any degree, is a modal property of merely instrumental treatment.[1] It is a matter of what the agent would do under certain conditions, not a matter of what the agent is doing. A common case of readily reversible conduct is action that is "out of character." Where this occurs, the normal motivational elements in the agent's character may intervene on the slightest reminder of the deviation from the person's norm. The memory of promises, the constraints that go with friendship, or the thought of a beclouded future may come quite unbidden. External elements, such as social pressure, can also lower the threshold for reversal.

We should also consider non-modal properties of such treatment: *constraints* (of a certain kind—many are of course modal). Merely instrumental treatment, even in a callous person, can be constrained by, for instance, a standing desire to avoid being criticized. For some who are treating others merely as means, constraints of prudence or civility may affect the manner of the treatment, for instance by moderating the tone of criticism. At a single time, then, merely instrumental motivation can fully explain why an action (say criticizing a decision) is *performed,* while its *manner* (say as

1. I am intentionally speaking as if merely instrumental treatment always *is* reversible in principle. If this is questionable, it is for cases that are at best rare and do not concern our discussion of normal human agents.

civil) may be explained by prudential motivation or a habit of civility or both. The former explainers are purposive and explain why the agent *does* the thing in question; the latter are adverbial and explain why the action is performed in the *way* (or some way) that it is. In rough terms, motivators of action drive it; constraints on action modulate it.

As with purposive explainers of action, then, we must recognize potential as well as actual constraints on action. Suppose that, in criticizing someone, I am not constrained by civility or prudence and speak in a rude tone. If someone I respect were to say that I was behaving rudely, I would be embarrassed and would likely moderate my tone.[2] Perhaps, however, as in Nazi "medical" experiments, someone could treat a person both entirely without such constraints and, relative to any civilizing influences that can be brought to bear, irreversibly. If there is no reversal world here, such persons might be said to be *essentially* evil: evil in any world in which they exist. A gravely evil tendency would be part of their very nature.

Two kinds of (actual) constraints have been implicitly distinguished. We might call them *active* and *passive*. Both can be manifestations of a single trait of character or of a virtue or of combinations of traits or virtues. Constraints of civility and of good manners, for instance, are active when one effortfully holds back an angry response because it is rude;

---

2. Alternatively, criticism of my rude manner might cause me to think of and *become motivated by* a previously unnoticed benefit I could give the person I am treating merely as a means. Here, whether or not I alter the manner of my treatment, in doing the "same thing," such as issuing criticism, I no longer treat the person *merely* as a means. In embodying a new purposive explainer of the action, this case is like that of reversibility; but it differs in that the same action continues. Merely instrumental treatment, then, is relative to time.

they are passive when one is having an ordinary conversation that touches on something divisive and, since one does not know the other person well, spontaneously keeps the conversation light, in line with one's habits for managing delicate situations. No effort need be exercised; the constraint may operate in an automatic way. In treating someone merely as a means, the agent is both unconcerned—at the time—with anything not taken to be instrumentally relevant to the end, and is *either* unconstrained by any such thing—whether actively or passively—or constrained only out of self-interest or some other motive consistent with relating to the person in a way that takes the other's instrumental role in achieving the end as overriding any competing motivation. This kind of unconcern and this limitation on constraints help to bring out the force and moral relevance of the 'merely' in 'treating merely as a means'.

It is not easy to specify what constitutes either kind of constraint, and it may be preferable to speak of active constraints as *occurrent*, since they are operative in influencing behavior at the time in question and tend to manifest themselves in consciousness, say through a focused effort of which the agent is aware, whereas the passive ones tend not to manifest themselves in consciousness. We might, then, call the passive constraints *dispositional*; their role is not occurrent but subliminal and, in a related sense, implicit. *Some* degree of constraint is implicit in being motivated by a consideration not instrumentally relevant to one's end, say by standards of etiquette applying to how one asks an employee to do something. But constraint does not imply motivation, as opposed to potential for motivation, to act in the alternative way in question.

Consider a case in which a student whispers audibly while a classmate is speaking. Suppose that I am the instructor and warn the student, citing guidelines for classroom discussion. I am passively constrained by a standard of respect for persons in how I do this; I need not have any specific desire to treat the student with respect in so doing. A constraint does, however, imply a *disposition* to be occurrently motivated. If, for instance, I must twice ask the student to be quiet on the same day, this constraint may become active. Being annoyed, I now make an *effort* (hence am occurrently motivated) to choose a respectful warning; through this effort, I observe the constraint and am able to be polite.

III. Motivation and Constraints in the Appraisal of Character

We can better see the importance of motivating and constraining elements by considering three points about their role in moral appraisal of persons and their actions. One concerns motivation; the second concerns moral character; the third concerns constraints as related to both.

First, as to the motivation that purposively explains conduct, any purposive explanation of action provides a path that connects the action with character, in the broad sense of *psychological constitution* at the time. The connection may well be to a trait of character, such as greed; but an agent's purpose, say to get confidential information, will at least be part of the agent's motivational character at the time regardless of any connection of the relevant desires and beliefs to any enduring trait.

Second—and this point is important in any virtue ethics—*moral* character *is* in part a matter of what *kinds* of motives do or (under relevant conditions) would explain our treatment of others and, if we should treat them merely instrumentally, of how *readily* we would reverse course given a reason to do so. Our moral character is also a matter of the strength in us of the constraints of civility, veracity, fairness, and other constraints. Roughly speaking, constraints of these kinds narrow both the territory and manner in which one even *can* treat others merely as means. As later chapters will bring out further, the wide-ranging constraints of respect for persons impose limitations of substance concerning what sorts of deeds one can do toward them; and the constraints of civility impose limitations mainly on the manner in which one acts toward others, insofar as that is separable from the deeds themselves. An agent's readiness to respond to new considerations is important not only in appraising character—including the constraints internal to it—but also in distinguishing the two kinds of merely instrumental treatment we have been comparing: the reversible and the irreversible. Other things equal, irreversible merely instrumental conduct is morally worse than the reversible kind, and merely instrumental conduct that more nearly approaches irreversibility is worse than merely instrumental conduct that is closer to reversibility.[3]

Third, regarding constraints, we have already seen how moral character is partly a matter of what does or would constrain both what we do toward others and *how* we do it. Here is another aspect of the point, bearing on degree of moral deficiency. Consider a manager's giving scathing criticism to an employee merely to cause anger that would yield resignation. If the merely instrumental treatment is also given in an objectionable *way*, say so loudly as to be unnecessarily

---

3. The points I make here about character presuppose that there is such a thing and that traits of character, or at least elements therein, have some descriptive and explanatory importance. I cannot here appraise the "situationist" critique of character ethics, but many points in this chapter and others bear on how to respond to it. For a detailed discussion pertinent to developing such a response see Pauline Kleingeld, "Consistent egoists and situation managers: Two problems for situationism," forthcoming in *Philosophical Explorations* (2015).

overheard, it is important how readily the agent will favorably alter the manner of action. Even when an action, such as
criticizing an employee, is justified, the lack of certain constraints that commonly go with treating someone merely as
a means can be morally important as indicating a defect in
character. The capacity for constraint, then, like the capacity
for overriding motives that stop or reverse merely instrumental conduct, is important both in appraising character and
in distinguishing between treatment merely as a means that
is (favorably) alterable in manner and merely instrumental treatment that is not thus alterable. Again, other things
equal, the latter is morally worse.

Constraints of morality, empathy, civility, and simple
decency are common, but in special cases they can be con-
sciously resisted. Shakespeare's *Macbeth* contains a memora-
bly vivid description of forswearing constraints. Here is Lady
Macbeth's chilling resolution:

> ... Come, you spirits
> That tend on mortal thoughts, unsex me here,
> And fill me, from the crown to the toe, topfull
> Of direst cruelty! Make thick my blood ...
> That no compunctious visitings of nature
> Shake my fell purpose ... Come, thick night
> And pall thee in the dunnest smoke of Hell,
> That my keen knife not see the wound it makes,
> Nor Heaven peer through the blanket of the dark
> To cry "Hold, hold."
>
> *(Act 1, scene 5, 41–55)*

If her invocation had succeeded, she would have been even
more willing to use merely as means anyone protecting the
coveted throne. Her words bring out both what would constitute merely instrumental treatment and why, morally, it well
serves as a kind of negative ideal. Merely instrumental conduct toward others is incongruous with virtue and, though it

does not by itself entail vice, it may still be among the clearest manifestations of it.

———

Persons, like material objects, can be treated as means. But, unlike material objects (some would say 'other material objects'), persons should never be treated merely as means—or so our examples seem to show. This is not to suggest anything about how often they actually are so treated; that is a question for the social psychology of ethics. So is the question how often ordinary people *approach* treating others merely as means. Approaching it can be reprehensible too, though less so than conduct that fully constitutes merely instrumental treatment.

We have also seen that, in a given case of merely instrumental treatment or of conduct approaching it, people may be more or less constrained and their conduct may also be more or less readily reversible. These matters of degree are left open by what I have said. Our discussion also leaves open much else: exactly what factors constrain normal interpersonal relations, how strong different kinds tend to be, and what types of acts might constitute, or partly constitute, merely instrumental treatment. The next chapter will show several ways in which the notion of merely instrumental treatment is more complex than that of action, even that of what we do intentionally, which does not include all action. Treating someone merely as a means, we shall find, has other dimensions, both motivational and behavioral.

3

ACTION, TREATMENT, AND CONDUCT

The examples we have considered leave no doubt that merely instrumental treatment is a morally significant kind of conduct. In partial summary of the account so far developed, we might say that treating a person merely as a means is doing something toward that person (1) on the basis of instrumental motivation, i.e., in order to realize a further end (in this case one to which the person is seen as instrumental), (2) with no motivational concern, and a disposition not to acquire such a concern, regarding any non-instrumental aspects of the action(s), and (typically) (3) in the absence of certain kinds of constraints.[1] The stronger the negative disposition, the less nearly reversible is the treatment and the less effective any relevant cooperative constraints tend to be. Moreover, a major element in at least the paradigm cases is a kind of callous indifference, often a recalcitrant indifference, to any non-instrumental considerations (apart from certain selfish ones). This indifference may be manifested

1. Examples to be given below will illustrate the possibility that with a certain kind of motivation an action could be merely instrumental, yet constrained in a way that makes it appear altruistic. Constraints are not as such motivators of the action they constrain, and the good influence they may have on the manner of its performance cannot eliminate every motivational ground of action that renders it merely instrumental.

in the manner of action as well as in its type. In manner, an action may be (for instance) crude, manipulative, deceitful, or hurtful, and the indifference that goes with merely instrumental treatment extends to valuational and moral considerations, such as the good of the person or any obligation to be considerate.[2]

This last point may seem to imply that the concept of treating someone merely as a means is valuational after all and so cannot serve as a descriptive basis for moral judgment. But, although valuational and moral considerations are among the non-instrumental elements to which treating someone merely as a means implies indifference, the concept of so treating someone does not essentially involve them. They may be invoked to clarify it by contrast, but they are not constituents in it. The *reference* of 'non-instrumental elements' is indefinitely wide; but the concept is specified by the descriptive notions of producing an effect, instrumental motivation, and other psychological notions, such as that of *not* pursuing something for its own sake.[3]

2. This account avoids the counterexamples brought by Derek Parfit and Samuel J. Kerstein against other accounts of merely instrumental treatment. See Parfit's *On What Matters* (Oxford: Oxford University Press, 2011), 2 vols., 1: 212–228; and Kerstein's "Treating Others Merely as Means," *Utilitas* 21, 2 (2009), 163–180. The rough account of treating merely as a means Parfit offers (p. 228) differs from mine and is less detailed, but discussing the differences is not necessary in this book. Kerstein does not offer a positive account in that paper, but does in his *How to Treat Persons* (Oxford: Oxford University Press, 2013), esp. ch. 3. This book also contains plausible informative responses to Parfit's account and a wealth of examples bearing both on using people and on the notion of treating them merely as means.

3. A related point is that treatment of a person merely as a means is possible for someone amoral. This is an important point about it—and about some amoral people. It does not show that the

I. Action, Endeavor, and Consequence

Much of what we do is not morally important, but almost everyone does many things that are. Morally important doings are typically actions. Actions are roughly things agents do that are intentional under some description.[4] Intentional action, in turn, is roughly action performed for a reason, but here we need not attempt a full-scale account of doing or of intentional action. It will suffice to clarify these notions to the extent necessary for explicating the treatment of persons.

It is already evident in what has been said—and will be more so as we proceed—that treatment of persons is not a matter of just any kind of action in relation to them. But action

concept of treating merely as a means is non-moral, since a concept can apply to an agent who does not use it (or even have it); but it does show that treating someone merely as a means does not entail applying (or exercising) moral concepts. It is less clear that the latter point holds for treating persons as ends. The account of that concept in Part II will suggest that it does. I should add something implicit in the role given in chapter 1 to non-instrumental desire. The disposition is to be understood (as it normally would be) intentionalistically: it is toward what the agent *takes* not to be instrumentally relevant (though not necessarily under that description), and this leaves room for factual mistakes.

4. Granted, a physician could ask what an unconscious patient is doing, and this could be both non-intentional "all the way down," i.e., have no description under which it is intentional, and still morally important, as where the patient is the president and the doings indicate that a successor should now be named. The formulation in the text is not intended as an analysis, but should serve the purposes of this book. For an analysis I consider approximately adequate, see my "Acting for Reasons," *Philosophical Review* XCV, 4 (1986), 511–546; and for extensive discussion of reasons, especially in relation to normativity, see Parfit, *On What Matters*.

is plainly a necessary element in such treatment. Indeed, it is natural to *name* an instance of treatment of a person using an act-description, say, inviting, criticizing, assisting, animatedly greeting, reprimanding sharply, or simply ignoring. None of these represents *basic action,* i.e., action performed "at will": directly and not *by* performing some other action. We greet by, for instance, saying 'hello' or extending a hand (or both); reprimand by issuing critical remarks; ignore by avoiding eye contact; and so forth.[5] The range of acts basic for us (performable at will) is commonly very wide.

A non-basic action may have more than one basic action as a behavioral "root." This is illustrated by the twofold greeting: by simultaneous word and handshake. Moreover, treatment may have many constituent actions, some basic, some not. Treatment may thus be multiplex: it may be realized by more than one action or activity at a time, as where a choral conductor treats the singers harshly by violently moving the baton while scowling and singing a phrase in a corrective

5. Compare speaking of an agent's doing one thing by doing another, even when this relation is grounded in a single basic action. This is often more convenient than talk of doing a single thing that bears the relevant descriptions. By ordering a soldier to do something, an officer may endanger the soldier; but this can also be put in terms of the officer's doing something basically, like ordering the soldier to rush the enemy, which also bears the description 'endangering the soldier'. This latter, "coarse-grained" way to individuate actions is often called the Anscombe-Davidson way. See G. E. M. Anscombe, *Intention,* 2nd ed. (Oxford: Blackwell, 1963) and Donald Davidson, *Essays on Actions and Events* (Oxford: Oxford University Press, 1980). The most detailed action-theoretic development of the fine-grained approach is probably Alvin I. Goldman's *A Theory of Human Action* (Englewood Cliffs, NJ: Prentice-Hall, 1970). I do not presuppose the ultimate preferability of either approach, though the coarse-grained view best fits my theory.

tone. Moreover, a single action or a unified set of actions may (partly) constitute more than one kind of treatment. Reprimanding may be an instance of treating fairly, treating candidly, treating deftly—and also of treating as a means, whether merely so or not. It may be treating fairly on the basis of justice, deftly on the basis of cautious wording, and instrumentally on the basis of a need to display an example to would-be offenders. Treatment of persons, then, can simultaneously realize a plurality of treatment-types.

Reprimanding may also be basically or non-basically performed: basically, if at will one simply blurts out one's immediate thought that (e.g.) 'You had no right to do that', but non-basically if one chooses one's action, where the choice is a basic selection of wording (a mental action), and, *by* writing one's words down (done by basically moving one's hand), issues a reprimand (where such reprimanding is a non-basic action). There are various reasons, some moral, some pragmatic, some whimsical, for using one action-description or another to specify treatment of a person. Commonly, this description is selected to capture the most salient element in the treatment. The action (or group of related actions) in question is what I propose to call the *vehicle* of the treatment: roughly, the action(s) such that the treatment is constituted by the agent's performing it (or them) for a certain kind of reason and in a certain way. This conception of treatment will be developed in this chapter and further in later ones.

Among the sources of treatment-descriptions are categories of moral obligation. This should be no surprise: if how we treat persons is of high moral importance, it is to be expected that the modes of treatment are manifested by ways of doing things that are the main kinds of objects of obligation and prohibition. These negative and positive obligations prominently include those of justice and non-injury, veracity and fidelity, beneficence and self-improvement, reparation and gratitude, and liberty and respectfulness.[6] Included, then, among corresponding treatment-descriptions, are 'treating her fairly', 'treating him honestly', 'treating him ungratefully', 'making amends', 'holding him captive', and 'treating them disrespectfully'. These expressions are apparently based on thinking of conduct (at least partly) in one or more of these widely known ethical categories. But aesthetic categories may also figure, as where someone is said to have treated an author delicately or, regarding a composition sent for editing, to have revised it elegantly. There is no limit to the kinds of act-types that can serve as vehicles of treatment, and moral appraisal should take account of this variety, in ways that will shortly become apparent.

It will help to make three further preliminary points about the kind of descriptions of behavior we need to understand if we are to appreciate the complexity and appraisal of treatment.

First, treatment can be described, though not explicated or fully specified, in terms of *trying*. Trying is a matter of what the agent is aiming to bring about. Thus, one could answer 'what was it about his treatment of her that disturbed you?' with 'he was trying to intimidate her'. Here no vehicle of the intermediary treatment (the action or actions representing the attempt to intimidate) is specified. This hampers, even if it does not entirely prevent, assessment of the agent's conduct. 'Trying' is a higher-order act-description: it entails

6. The first eight items on this list are those stressed by W. D. Ross in his widely discussed *The Right and the Good* (Oxford: Oxford University Press, 1930). See his ch. 2 and my *The Good in the Right: A Theory of Intuition and Intrinsic Value* (Princeton, NJ: Princeton University Press, 2004), which, esp. in ch. 5, clarifies Ross's list and adds two obligations of the same kind. One, that of respectfulness, corresponds to the obligations of manner in acting that are extensively considered in this book.

doing something *purposively*—endeavoring to achieve the end indicated by the object of the trying, say, *to intimidate*; but calling behavior trying to intimidate (or, e.g., intimidating treatment) does not specify what action the agent aims at realizing that end.

Second, treatment can be described *consequentially*—roughly, in terms of what the agent is bringing about or affecting by it. One person might actually be intimidating another in talking a certain way. If we assume intentional action, as with purposive descriptions, we may see what end is attributed—intimidation—but not by what means. We again have a higher-order description whose application entails the performance of at least one action but does not specify any particular action.

The third point is evident in this and other cases we have considered: treatment may be temporally extended or, less commonly, instantaneous. It may be as extended as holding someone captive or as brief as face-slapping. Given how extended conduct can be, its motivation, manner, or both can change. A guard could for days hold me captive merely to follow orders and might treat me harshly the whole time. Later, when the orders expire, the guard may find a different instrumental reason, say to collect ransom or, even over the same period, may also develop an affection for me and so be acting partly from end-regarding motives. Over time, motives underlying the same extended action, pattern of action, or activity can arise, intensify, weaken, mix, and disappear.

II. Two Levels of Behavioral Description

Treating people merely as means typically bespeaks callousness, and conduct that fits this pejorative instrumental description is prima facie wrong—wrong overall if there is no conflicting consideration of at least equal weight—thus, in another terminology, *wrong-making.* One might think, then (from reading Kant and others), that the act-*type* in question, the vehicle of the treatment, such as reprimanding—or indeed any act-type partly constituting the treatment—must be (prima facie) wrong, as are bullying, lying, and promise-breaking. But consider two cases in which, to save the regiment, Jack, a field commander, sends Juan on a dangerous mission. (We could also speak of ordering him to go on a dangerous mission, and there are other things roughly equivalent to doing this that Jack may be described as intentionally doing.) In the first case, glad of the chance to endanger the soldier, Jack—in intentionally doing the deed for the reason he does it, and in the way he does—treats Juan merely as a means. For him, Juan is just a military tool. Hence, given the force of 'merely' here, Jack is quite ready to let him suffer. In the second case, by contrast, momentarily acting purely as a strategist, Jack sends Juan on the mission only (solely), but not merely, as a means to saving the regiment. He may thus be acting within—with a certain sensitivity to—safety concerns. If they sufficiently constrain him, his conduct in sending Juan may not be reprehensible.

The conduct bears different morally relevant descriptions in the two cases depending on the agent's aims and dispositions. Treating Juan only as a means need not be reprehensible; treating him merely as a means is.[7] Granted, even if the conduct, as merely instrumental, is (prima facie)

7. Must Jack, be described as *acting wrongly*? This phrase can be ambiguous; it can mean instantiating an act-type that is wrong in the circumstances', but also, as the adverbial element suggests, 'doing something in the wrong *way*'. In the first sense it does not apply to Jack; in the second, it may. His conduct is reprehensible on the second count. Cf. Parfit, op. cit. (p. 216), where he uses 'acting wrongly' in the former way with no indication of possible ambiguity. Kerstein seems willing to do likewise; see, e.g., *How to Treat Persons*, p. 54.

reprehensible, it does not follow that the action of sending Juan is *on balance* wrong; with many lives as stake, it might be even worse not to send him at all. Then there is a reason to send him that is strong enough to outweigh endangering him. A given quite permissible type of act can be instantiated in a way that represents either kind of treatment and thereby is a vehicle of either permissible or impermissible conduct.

Another way to see the moral importance of merely instrumental treatment is to shift our focus from appraising actual conduct to decision making. Imagine not two ways in which Juan is treated by Jack but instead Jack's having two about equally good candidates for the dangerous mission: Juan and Pete. Jack might well be able to foresee that, being happy to have a chance to endanger Juan, he would likely be sending Juan merely as a means, whereas, with no dislike of Pete, he would be sending him only as one of the best candidates to do the job, though still as a means (and perhaps solely as such) to get the job done. Whether or not Jack himself employs the *concept* of merely instrumental treatment, he should foresee that he would have a prejudice in sending Juan and that he should neither indulge it nor risk its affecting what he might do if, for instance, Juan needs costly support. In this fact about himself, he has reason to prefer sending Pete. Merely instrumental treatment, then, has *prospective moral force*; its potential applicability affects moral responsibility for making good decisions and not just how we should appraise actual conduct.

Such cases suggest something often unclear in literature touching on merely instrumental treatment: that treating persons merely as means is not adequately explicable by appeal to the relevant act-types, those constituting the (or a) vehicle of the treatment. Indeed, no ordinary act-type is *intrinsically* a case of merely instrumental treatment. Treating merely as a means is a kind of conduct, and the concept of such treatment is both higher-level and double-barreled: *higher-level* because it does not specify an act-type, though its instantiation entails that there is an act-type (fitting a lower-level description) in virtue of whose instantiation—in the relevant way—the agent treats someone merely as a means; *double-barreled* because it both reports some action and implies a certain sort of motivational explanation of the action. Thus, 'merely as a means' has both behavioral and motivational elements, but implies nothing specific about what the act-type is.[8] There are, to be sure, ordinary (though not necessarily "simple") act-types—say lying, cheating, and stealing—whose instantiations commonly are or approach treating someone merely as a means, but no act-type of this kind is such that a token of it *must* constitute so treating someone.

III. Conduct as a Morally Important Category

Imagine that, after sending Juan on a dangerous mission, Jack is criticized by a fellow officer for egregious conduct. A natural defense might be that Juan is one of the soldiers most likely to get information needed to save the regiment. If the other officer is using 'conduct' as I am, in the sense encompassing treatment, one reply to Jack might be 'Yes, but you have it in for him, didn't warn him of the dangers, and would have let him suffer if he ran into trouble'. The complaint, then, is not about the action of sending Juan on the

---

8. I presuppose no account of levels of act-describing notions. There are, e.g., many ways to cheat. Is the notion of cheating a higher-level act-describing notion or just a quite unspecific one? And is any act-type intuitively *first*-level? Moving a finger is basic, and in that way, first-level, for most people and is the kind of act from which many others are "built." Devising a theory of levels is difficult, but nothing important in this book hinges on just how we structure this theory. For a useful account of levels of action, see Goldman, op. cit.

mission. Sending him may be within the officer's rights and quite proper. The complaint is not even to the effect that Juan is sent *in order to* put him at risk, since that is not Jack's purpose; the motivational element in the complaint concerns the officer's disposition not to protect him if danger should arise and hinder his instrumental effectiveness. This complaint also goes with the disapproval of the *manner* of the order: Juan is dispatched both "uncautioningly" and in a way that discourages resistance or questions. Jack might have a justification for not warning Juan, perhaps to avoid frightening him, but the point is that at least two elements in the treatment of Juan, its motivation and manner, need defense. Even if both are ethically defensible and within Jack's rights, the motivation of the command is at best tainted with the hope of (say) injury or death for the soldier, and the treatment still approaches using the soldier merely as a means even if the action that is its vehicle is quite in order. The case illustrates, then, that treatment has (at least) three significant dimensions, that it can be criticizable on the basis of any of them, and that it can be morally objectionable even when the action that is its vehicle is morally justified.

Treatment as Conduct

We should ask, then, why, since treating someone merely as a means is not constituted by "ordinary," prima facie wrong act-types such as lying, cheating, and slapping, it is morally objectionable conduct. In broad terms, the answer begins with the point that conduct constituting treating someone merely as a means has, in that very fact, a wrong-making property. The relevant act is performed both on the basis of a certain kind of motivational and cognitive grounding—such as a desire for credit with someone who can advance one's interests and a belief that falsely claiming to have given much to charity will get it—and with a disposition not to be concerned with any non-instrumental aspects of the treatment, such as resulting misfortune for the other person.[9] This disposition need not be reflected in actual desires concerning the other; it is (as a virtue ethicist might stress) something like a state of character and may be determined by, for instance, strongly predominant self-interested desires.[10]

The state of character underlying merely instrumental treatment merits criticism, but that is not the point here. Merely instrumental treatment represents voluntary action that is based on elements in that state; and (apart from compulsion, which would be excusatory) the agent acts with

9. The term 'resulting' is significant: an agent could treat someone merely as a means in doing one thing, say borrowing money, even though the agent has desires in another matter, such as a joint project, that would prevent so treating the person in that other connection. These other desires could reverse the merely instrumental treatment, e.g. where the agent realizes that callous deceit in borrowing may undermine the joint project. It should be clear, however, that, because of its double-barreled character, treating merely as a means, though its instantiation entails that of an act-type, is not itself an act-type, much less a basic one. This double-barreled character opens the way for a single act to be the vehicle of more than one instance of treatment. Assigning a task to Juan can be the vehicle both of unfair treatment of him (as done from dislike rather than justly, as by lottery or alternation of risky assignments with other capable soldiers) and preferential treatment of Pete, as deliberately sparing him danger.

10. This is a good place to note a distinction I observe here and will elaborate later (one I take to be available to, even if not explicitly drawn by, Kantian and other moral theorists). It is between a notion's being moral in *upshot* and moral in *content* (and similarly for the normative). If, e.g., treating someone merely as a means clearly and a priori entails its being prima facie wrong, the notion is moral in upshot. But neither its content nor the basic criteria for its application are moral.

responsibility for the overall resulting conduct. It is as if one drove too fast for safety in a residential neighborhood, willing to frighten or even hit someone who gets in the way and using, merely as a means of avoiding a traffic fine, the presence of a physician who happens to be on an emergency call and can explain that to the police. Even if nobody who can judge one's speed is present and one believes no one will get in the way, there is a certain behavioral momentum that one should have prevented. Merely instrumental treatment represents a momentum of the wrong kind, even if that momentum is indiscernible in the overt action that is its vehicle.

Motivation in the Constitution of Treatment and Action

Suppose that what is morally objectionable in treating people merely as means is partly due to the agent's underlying motivational constitution, even if a momentary state. Does this imply that we have obligations to act-from-particular-motives, say benevolence? I do not think so and I doubt we have such obligations.[11] Indeed, on my view

11. I have defended Kant (or at least one Kantian view) on the point in ch. 3 of *Practical Reasoning and Ethical Judgment* (London: Routledge, 2006), which suggests that although he took the moral worth of a deed to depend on the agent's motivation, he is not thereby committed to our having direct voluntary control of what motives determine our action. Some reasons why he might be thought to be so committed are found in Mary Glover, "Obligation and Value," *Ethics* 49, 1 (1938), 69–80, to which I have responded on the point in "Mary Glover on Obligation and Value," *Ethics* 125 2 (2015), 125–129. Granted, that we ought (as he requires) to act *on* a certain kind of maxim implies that we can at least *indirectly* bring this about. But this is a different point. Regarding the idea that we can directly (at will) act-on-a-particular-motive, I argue against

'acting for R', where R is a reason for which the person acts, does not stand for an action-description, and what it designates is not something an agent does—though it of course indicates action—namely, one or another deed based on R. The expression, like 'acting to bring about E', where E is an end, is a hybrid: saying that an agent acted for R (e.g. to keep a promise) answers two quite different questions: What did the agent do? and Why did the agent do it? The first question can be correctly answered only by specifying an action (or at least a doing conceived as manifesting agency); the second is typically and most explicitly answered by citing a motivating desire or a guiding belief, normally in a way that indicates both. The questions are radically different; and a statement that answers both is on that count a kind of hybrid that should not be taken to answer just one of them. Indeed, 'The agent A-ed for R', like 'The agent A-ed in order to bring about E', is equivalent to the compound 'The agent A-ed *and* the (or a sufficient) reason for the action was R' (or to bring about E). The statement indicates an action; but, unlike a report simply of what someone did, it also indicates an explanation of the action.[12]

Granted, a compound state of affairs such as contributing to a charity *and* doing it in order to fulfill a pledge might still be produced by simply doing the deed in question, particularly if bringing about this state of affairs is of a special kind. Suppose, for instance, I *have* only one reason, R, to A,

this below and, in more detail, in "Doxastic Voluntarism and the Ethics of Belief," *Facta Philosophica* 1, 1 (1999), which provides a partial account of the scope of voluntariness.

12. A particularly clear case of taking such descriptions as designating an action is Mary Glover's view that a surgeon's operating "because it is a duty" "is not the same act as to do it from [out of] a purely sadistic motive." See her study of Kant in contrast to Ross in "Obligation and Value,"69–80.

and I can *A* now. If I then decide to *A* and do it, I will in effect bring it about *that I A-ed for R*, which might be broadly considered a behavioral state of affairs. But this does not make *A*-ing for *R* an action. The point is that I had no way to do the deed *other* than for the one reason I had; thus, by doing it at all, I naturally bring about my doing it for that reason. But as the 'by' indicates, the compound state of affairs, *A-ing for R*, still seems non-basically produced. In any case, it remains true that the deed I do is one thing, what I bring about by doing it is another, and what explains it is still another and is in a different category—that of intentionality rather than that of behavior—as where the act is explained by an intention to achieve something.

All this is compatible with the point that we have enough capacity to understand why we do what we do toward others, and why we *intend* to do it (or are motivated to do it), to enable us often to tell whether we are *tempted* to treat them merely as means—or in any other way to act wrongly toward them. Partly for this reason, we can often abstain from so doing, as Socrates is reported to have done (though resisting a different kind of reprehensible motivation) when he said to a boy, "I would beat you if I were not angry."[13] Such *abstention* from reprehensible conduct, unlike acting-from-a-particular-motive, *is* something we can commonly do at will. We are fallible about our motivation; but this shows at most that we may be *excusable* for merely instrumental treatment, not that it is not prima facie wrong. On the whole, it is a kind of conduct we can make ourselves indisposed toward in the first place and can usually abstain from if we find ourselves leaning toward it.

13. This attribution is from Seneca, *On Anger*, chapter. 15, paragraph 3, but I have it on good authority that the line is not found in Plato and may be from Xenophon.

Calling merely instrumental treatment *conduct* marks a distinction that befits its higher-level, multidimensional character. It also indicates a contrast both with appraisals of character as a (normally) long-term cluster of traits, and with assessments of intentional actions conceived as a kind of tokening of act-types: roughly, as doings that are, under some description, intentional. The thing done is an act (or activity) of a certain act-type, but *simply* performing an act of that type never by itself constitutes merely instrumental treatment. We could call such treatment 'behavior', but this term does not imply motivation and can designate non-intentional acts. In one use, 'conduct' has both the required specificity and the needed breadth. This makes it apt for various ethical purposes, both descriptive and evaluative. As is now evident, I am using it mainly to refer to certain acts or activities performed for a reason, in a certain way; and I presuppose that conduct occurs under certain conditions, where these conditions may include morally significant elements such as the agent's self-awareness.[14] Morally bad conduct may, for instance, be doing something of a (prima facie) wrongful *type, for* a selfish reason, and *in* a callous way, and may occur under conditions that allow the agent to abstain or redirect the agent's behavior.

Conduct may be bad, however, morally or in other ways, on account of any of the three kinds of broadly behavioral variables indicated in many of our examples: act-type, motivation, and manner in which the (or a) constituent action is performed. It is true that, often, the manner in which an action is performed is utterly unremarkable; but one could

14. Not just any act or activity fitting this description is naturally called *conduct,* but although the term normally implies doings viewed evaluatively, it need not be morally normative and does not imply any specific evaluation.

do even a clearly right thing in a way so callous that even with an appropriate motive underlying the deed, the conduct is morally criticizable. I might be obligated to inform someone of the untimely death of a brother. Doing this is the right deed, but it would be wrong to do it in coarse, vivid language of a kind that might wound the sensibilities of someone hearing this even about a stranger. The manner in which we do things can reveal much about us, it can profoundly affect others, and it can deserve praise or merit blame.

Conduct, then, is more complex than action narrowly conceived, but it is still broadly behavioral; and although it often reveals more about character than action by itself does, it is not a feature of character. It is, moreover, an element in our manifest accomplishments in a way traits of character are not. This places it between elements of character on the dispositional side and overt performances on the behavioral side. Conduct requires action, but is not a matter simply of the type of act the treatment embodies.

IV. Manners of Action versus Actions as Defined by Manner

As to the contrast between conduct and action taken by itself, simply as an instantiation of an act-type, it is true that we can give a behavioral name to an act-type instantiated in a certain way, and many act-describing terms apparently reflect a sense of the importance of some of these two-dimensional types. To yell, for instance, is to speak very loudly in a certain way; to pace is to walk in a certain repetitive way. Here the act-types are *essentially mannered*. Instances must be quite specific and describable by a quite specific adverb, whereas many act-types, such as writing, traveling, and even greeting, are not essentially tied to any specific manner of action or to particular basic acts (though, to any particular basic action, many adverbs will apply). Nonetheless, even yelling and

pacing can themselves be done in different ways. In practice, there are limits to the number of ways we can control
the manner of our actions; but for a huge range of act-types
that we can consider realizing—including essentially mannered actions—*how* we should do the thing in question is
morally significant. If, however, an act-type instantiated in
a certain way can in principle be described using a single
action-designating term, why need we take the manner of
action to be crucial for conduct conceived as an independent
variable? Why not simply rename the act and appraise as a
unit the action so designated?

To answer this, recall yelling and pacing. Can we *understand* these act-types apart from understanding the action
that, when performed in the relevant *manner,* justifies our
using the act-name in question? Surely such adverbial modi-
fiers of act-reports presuppose action of a variable kind; they
are not comprehensible apart from the modified action in
question, such as speaking or walking, and they do not function to yield a report merely of that action. 'She declined
politely' is not a primitive semantic unit designating an
act-type. It is not, for instance, just a stylistic variant of a
report of her declining. Indeed, our assessment of her behavior may turn on her manner of declining, say on the kind
of politeness it exhibits. Declining may be done flippantly.
Moreover, in principle the "new" action, declining politely,
can itself be performed in different ways, say dryly or apolo-
getically. Similarly, yelling may be done shrilly, and pacing
may be done rapidly. Shrill yelling may be done threaten-
ingly, rapid pacing rhythmically. In principle, no matter how
complex an action is, there will be more than one way it can
be performed. This applies even to actions that, like yelling,
are equivalent to adverbially modified basic actions (or more
nearly basic ones).

There are practical limits on the ways in which we can do
things. But none of the points emerging here undermines

the view that we often bear moral responsibility for the manner of our actions and that our conduct is characterized in part on the basis of that manner. To try to reduce descriptions of the manners of actions to reports of different actions unmodified by adverbs or equivalent qualifiers is to bury a morally significant ontological difference under a linguistic veil.[15]

The point that act-type does not by itself determine the conduct in question should perhaps be uncontroversial, but must be stressed. We should not deny that conduct itself is an instantiation of a kind of broadly behavioral type: there are *conduct-types*. But they are more complex than act-types. Conduct is not just instantiating an act-type; it is three-dimensional: *doing* something *for* a particular set of reasons and *in* a particular manner. But, in part because we have *indirect* control over why we do things—if only through our power to abstain from or delay doing them—and, within limits, over the manner of our action, conduct is subject to moral evaluation as part of our records as moral agents.

It should now be apparent how merely instrumental treatment of persons fits the three-dimensional account of conduct described in this chapter. Treating a person merely as a means is doing something toward that person in a certain

---

15. For considerations supporting this point, see Donald Davidson, "The Logical Form of Action Sentences," in his *Essays on Actions and Events*. It should be stressed that in the text I am speaking of adverbs of manner. There are other kinds, such as *adverbs of intentionality*, e.g. 'intentionally', 'deliberately', 'purposely', even 'knowingly'. Another category is closely related, e.g. 'accidentally', 'mistakenly', and 'unwittingly'; these may cancel some of the former set. The theory of adverbs is an important territory I cannot explore in detail here.

manner, on the basis of instrumental motivation, with no motivational concern regarding any non-instrumental aspects of the action(s), and with a disposition not to acquire such a concern. We bear responsibility for our conduct and not just for actions constituting its vehicle—the usually overt deeds that represent what, in a narrow sense, we are doing. If we do not in general have direct positive voluntary control of all the morally significant aspects of our conduct—such as why we engage in it—we commonly do have direct *negative* control of it: we can abstain from the action(s) at its core and thereby prevent the conduct. Moreover, we can also usually control its manner, at least by keeping it within constraints of civility. Even when the manner of an action is acceptable, merely instrumental treatment always has a negative moral status: an objectionable dispositional element that makes such conduct prima facie wrong, and there is often sufficient reason to abstain from it. Why that is so may already be evident, but there is much more to say about it, and explaining it in some detail is my next major concern.

4

THE WRONG-MAKING CHARACTER OF MERELY INSTRUMENTAL TREATMENT

We have seen that in treating someone merely as a means the agent need not be "doing something wrong," in the common sense of doing a deed that is wrong. Donating a large sum of money to a good cause when welcomed to do so by a representative of the cause is not wrong and might even be supererogatory, but it might also be a case of treating the person merely as a means to gain access to a higher official one wants to suborn. Here the grounding reason for the action is the main element that makes the conduct of which the action is the vehicle morally criticizable (which is not to deny that even the motive alone is a morally bad element in the agent). The manner of such an action might also count morally against the conduct: the gift could be made in an offensively patronizing way. To be sure, this kind of defect need have no implication of instrumental treatment: an objectionable manner of performance does not by itself imply a particular kind of motivation. End-regarding treatment can also occur in a morally criticizable manner, as will be more evident when we explore it in Part II. First, however, more must be said about what is ethically objectionable about treating persons merely as means.

I. Thick and Thin Moral Questions

Implicit in what we have seen is a point important for the appraisal of merely instrumental treatment. A wrong-making property of a type of conduct need not be behavioral, in the sense that it belongs to the relevant act-type, for instance beating, bullying, or lying. Suppose someone binds your wound, but merely to gain your trust in order to defraud you later. Even if the nursing is done with consummate skill, the conduct—as the doing of the deed *with* a certain kind of motivation, *in* a certain way, and in the *absence* of certain non-instrumental concerns—is prima facie wrong if it constitutes merely instrumental treatment. This is partly because of the reprehensible state of character—at least of motivational character at the time—underlying the deed. Being in such a state of character is bad in itself, but it is not an instance of conduct or even behavior. Still, to allow oneself to *express* bad character in action in the indicated way is to permit oneself to engage in morally bad conduct. More concretely, given that merely instrumental treatment embodies a disposition not to be concerned with any non-instrumental aspects of the action in question, it commonly exposes the person so treated to a risk of harm. In that way, the treatment is at least potentially harmful and, like bullying, it is sometimes plainly and frighteningly so. The greater the importance to the agent of the end to which someone is treated merely as a means, and the more hurting the other facilitates realizing the end, the more likely is the agent's doing such harm. It is surely plausible to believe that those who tend toward treating others merely as means are often among the callous agents quite willing to hurt others where it advances their own ends.

Acting Morally

The vocabulary of action contains a phrase that seems highly appropriate to conduct that is reprehensible despite the permissibility of the action that is its vehicle. Recall the deceptive nurse. In one use of the phrase, the nurse is *acting wrongly,* even though doing a *type* of deed (binding the wound) that is prima facie obligatory.[1] Even if, in the dimension of the manner of its execution—say, gentle and painless—the conduct is laudable, it still has a bad root: the desire to defraud you. Overall, then, the conduct is morally bad; and whether or not we say that the agent is acting

1. The phrase 'acting wrongly' is wider than 'doing something wrong'. This should not be a surprise given that plainly one can do a good deed in the wrong *way,* a case describable by adverbs. Where the overall conduct is wrong because of motive rather than manner, the term 'wrongly' is commonly appropriate, perhaps more so than where a wrongful deed is done. One example is found in Henry Sidgwick (though he does not indicate the difference). He says, of "a man who prosecutes from malice," that "he does not really act rightly; for, though it may be his duty to prosecute, he really ought not to do it from malice." See *The Methods of Ethics,* 7th ed. (London: Macmillan, 1907), 208. He also says (discussing gratitude) something concerning the manner of action: "Perhaps it makes a great difference whether the service be lovingly done: as in this case it seems inhuman [thus prima facie wrong?] that there should be no response of affection: whereas if the benefit be coldly given [thus in a wrongful manner?], the mere recognition of the obligation and the settled disposition to repay it seem to suffice" (op. cit., p. 260). Cf. Aristotle: "the just and temperate person is not the one who does them [just and temperate actions] merely, but the one who does them as [in the way] just and temperate people do" (*Nicomachean Ethics* 1105b, Crisp trans.); and "Nor is there a good or bad way to go about such things—committing adultery, say, with the right woman, or in the right place, or in the right way" (*NE* 1107a). The last use of 'way' seems to designate manner, but in any case Aristotle seems to have had a sense of the importance of this adverbial dimension of action.

wrongly, we can agree that the conduct is morally criticizable. This way of describing merely instrumental treatment suggests that the notion of such treatment may be important for virtue ethics as well as for Kantian and other ethical theories.

For a virtue ethicist, it might seem preferable to speak of a *bad*-making characteristic rather than a *wrong*-making one. Treating someone merely as a means typically reflects a kind of vice (or at least a temporary state akin to a persistent condition characteristic of someone having a relevant vice), and one might think that bad character—in the wide sense that includes the internal elements which indicate at least in part how the agent sees the action—rather than reprehensible conduct is the appropriate evaluative notion.

I grant the appropriateness of ascribing some kind of defect in character, assuming we can speak so where the defect may also be—as merely instrumental treatment certainly may be—"out of character." But the conduct in question is also morally objectionable, quite apart from the agent's overall character. Thus, although what is wrong-making in such treatment might be at least partially explained by a plausible virtue ethics, embracing virtue ethics is not needed to explain it. Recognizing conduct as an ethically significant category with three important moral dimensions does not require reliance on the notions of virtue or vice. The two ethical positions—the conduct theory and virtue ethics—agree, however, in rejecting any position implying that moral appraisal of agents directly applies to behavior *only* as instantiating an act-type. A lustrous deed may conceal callousness or even malice.

The Doing of Deeds

Conduct is a matter not just of what we do but also of why and how we do it. Given this three-dimensional character, the notion of conduct goes with a distinction between two kinds of ethical question, *thick* and *thin*. Thick questions are three-dimensional; thin questions are one-dimensional. Consider the hypocritical nurse. Asking whether the person *acted morally*, in the widest sense of the term,[2] or, more explicitly, whether the person's conduct was morally acceptable, is *fully* answered (positively) only by indicating (in relation to the circumtances of behavior) three things: that the act-type was permissible, its motivation appropriate in the context, and its manner of performance morally acceptable. Asking whether the agent did the right thing (or simply did right), by contrast, is a thin question: a full positive answer may consist simply in specifying a permissible act-type. Since the (or a) right thing can be done both for the wrong reason and in the wrong way, moral conduct is not achieved merely by doing the right thing.[3]

Thin ethical questions concern what deeds are to be done; thick questions concern the doing of them. Similarly, 'What should I do to (or with) *x*' (where *x* is a person), is, in many common contexts, thin compared with 'How should I treat *x*?' As many kinds of cases show, we can do the right thing even if the manner (or some other aspect) of our doing of it is wrong. The full breadth

2. If the metaphor of width is taken seriously, the question what kind of person one should be is even thicker, at least in that character traits are crucial for answering it, whereas the conduct question concerns the agent at a time or over an interval of activity, and need not presuppose that the determinative elements are traits of character.

3. I have previously introduced the distinction between thick and thin ethical questions in "Kantian Intuitionism as a Framework for the Justification of Moral Judgments," in *Oxford Studies in Normative Ethics*, vol. 2, ed. Mark Timmons (Oxford: Oxford University Press, 2012), 129–151.

of moral standards cannot be adequately appreciated without taking account of this point; and morally responsible regulation of our doings requires that, when we deliberate about what is the right thing to do—the right deed—we give due consideration not just to finding the right act-type but also to why, and how, we would be doing the deed in question. I may see that I must criticize an employee by pointing out a certain failing; but if, on the only occasion that will permit it, I foresee that I would be bitter and angry after a board meeting and would do it harshly or partly from a desire to "lash back at the world," then even though it is what I should do from the point of the view of the thin ethical question, asking the thick question will likely show me that my doing of it, my actual instantiating of the act-type, would not be good conduct. I might be doing a deed that is morally right, but not acting morally in doing it. Acting morally is not just a matter of doing morally permissible deeds.

Literary examples of acting morally, conceived as conduct, abound. Among the vivid pictures of the importance of how we do what we do is Shakespeare's description of the conduct of the Thane of Cawdor in his dying moments:

> He implored your Highness' pardon, and set forth
> A deep repentance. Nothing in his life
> Became him like the leaving it. He died
> As one who had been studied in his death.
>
> *(Macbeth, I, I, 6–9)*

We have here a picture of conduct in which, from a motive of remorse, and in a penitent manner, a man asks pardon. In his last moments, in the leaving of his life, he is acting repentantly and apparently trying, perhaps successfully, to act morally.

Two-Dimensional Questions

Where a concept is three-dimensional, philosophers may naturally ask what is to be made of the related one-dimensional and two-dimensional aspects of it. The one-dimensional questions that concern us are those regarding just act-type, just motivation, or just manner of performance. All of these are important. The theory of obligation concerns mainly act-types: what we may and may not do in the domain of action. The theory of moral worth—important in both virtue ethics and rule ethics[4]—concerns largely the appropriate kinds of motivation for action and aims at determining how the moral worth of an action is related to kinds of motivating reason. (The general theory of practical reason also encompasses accounts of, say, aesthetic, religious, and affectional worth.) As to the adverbial dimension, there is no conventional name for the theory of the *how* of action; but manners and styles of action are plainly open to appraisal, as indicated by some common uses of such questions as 'How did he treat you?', which do not concern motivation. I propose to speak of the *theory of moral manner* in reference to the task of determining standards for the how of action, for appropriate ways of doing what ought to be done. We also lack

4. The importance, for ethics, of moral worth, as well as its relation to the theory of obligation, are discussed in some detail in my "Acting from Virtue," *Mind* 104, 414 (1995), 449–71. For a study of the nature and importance of moral worth for Kant, and of his notion of acting from duty, see Philip Stratton-Lake, *Kant, Duty and Moral Worth* (London: Routledge, 2000). His interpretation of Kant makes room for manner of action to play a morally significant role but does not explicitly provide for it. The importance of manner of action may, however, be implicit in some of Kant's ethical writing and seems so in Aristotle's emphasis on the "way" virtuous actions are performed, e.g. in describing the just person; see, e.g., *Nicomachean Ethics*, 1105a and 1105b.

conventional names for the theory of the double-barreled questions of what an agent did *and* why or of what an agent did *and how*. Let us consider these two questions.

These double-barreled questions are important and moderately thick. Both virtue ethics and Kantian ethics have been heavily concerned with the why-question; but the how-question is also important. How we do what we do can make the difference between acting morally and acting immorally, even apart from why we do it. Who has not seen some actions, especially criticisms of others, performed in a way that makes them objectionable overall even if they are of a type, say indicating a series of someone's mistakes, that represents morally permissible action? This book focuses mainly on treatment as conduct and on the appraisal of conduct. It is often only two dimensions of an instance of conduct that are ethically significant, and it may be just one. Our discussion will bear on how to approach the moderately thick ethical questions; but it is the conduct question, the triple-barreled thick question about behavior, that most needs attention.

The proposed conception of conduct is consistent with the point that we have a degree of *indirect* voluntary control over aspects of our character and particularly over some important elements in us that may constrain our treatment of others.[5] This point is crucial for understanding the scope of moral judgment. What is *intrinsically* reprehensible about treating someone merely as a means is not the act-types that behaviorally manifest it; the act-types, unlike

---

5. A detailed discussion of responsibility for character is provided in my "Responsible Action and Virtuous Character," *Ethics* 101, 2 (1991), 304–321. My account distinguishes between *retrospective* responsibility for having done something and *prospective* responsibility for doing it, which, unlike the former, does not imply the act's performance. Neither kind, as applied to character, implies that we have direct control of it or even of our beliefs or desires.

lying and cheating—which are, to be sure, typical of such conduct—need not be prima facie wrong. Nor need the underlying motive(s) be reprehensible (as sections III and IV will show). What is intrinsically reprehensible is the merely instrumental conduct itself: the behavior constituted by the action *as* purposively explained by the merely instrumental motivation governing action, *as* performed with a disposition not to acquire any non-instrumental concern with the other person(s) in question, and *as* performed in a certain manner.

To illustrate, a given act-type, say employing someone to do a dangerous job, may be instantiated either in treating someone solely as a means *or* in treating someone merely as a means, depending on the agent's desires, beliefs, and motivational tendencies. Employing the person to do the job may be the right thing to do, but it may still be done for the wrong kind of reason. It may also be done in the wrong way. The action(s) constituting the vehicle of the conduct—the thing(s) done when, as in the examples of treatment offered so far, we speak of conduct in terms of the action(s), such as donating a sum, constituting its vehicle—must be performed in some way or other; but the manner of performance may or may not be noteworthy, and it is often not mentioned, whereas the moral appraisal of conduct must always explicitly take account of both act-type and reason(s) for the agent's doing a deed of that type. Conduct always occurs with some manner of action, but, more often than with act-type or motivation, the manner may be either morally unimportant or may not bear on whether the conduct is a case of merely instrumental or end-regarding treatment.

Conduct Considered Prospectively

So far, I have considered conduct mainly from a contemporaneous or retrospective point of view. But the prospective point of view is also important. We can often foresee whether we are inclined to treat someone merely as a means, or are moving toward such treatment. This is noteworthy in employment situations in which employers often have in mind a range of tasks to be required of the employee. Accordingly, we can often be expected to abstain from the relevant deeds. Where abstention is called for, we may be able to delegate to another person a deed we have reason to do, but cannot do in an appropriate way. This may result both in good conduct by our agent and avoiding bad conduct on our own part.

We can also learn—and teach children—not to relate to people in ways that foster merely instrumental treatment. There may, then, be actions an agent is responsible for in the background leading to merely instrumental treatment. Such actions may lie in the future as well as in the past. We are prospectively responsible for monitoring and even training ourselves, as well as retrospectively responsible for the type and manner of many deeds we have done. Prospective responsibility applies to all three dimensions of conduct: act-types, motivation, and manners of action.

Merely instrumental treatment, then, may reveal failure in taking prospective moral responsibility for specific past actions, as where someone manipulates others to cover up wrong-doing. This manipulation might have been avoidable by preventive action; the agent might, for instance, have abstained from entering a situation in which the temptation to treat someone merely as a means would be hard to resist. In this and other ways, we normally have a good measure of control over whether we engage in such treatment. But this element of control does not undermine the point that merely instrumental treatment is prima facie wrong on the basis of what it manifests about the motivational character of the agent at the time, and often (prima facie) wrong mainly on that basis. It may of course also be wrong by virtue of what we voluntarily do toward the person in question, particularly the act-type—such as defrauding or betraying—of the behavior constituting the vehicle of the conduct.

II. Substantive and Contrastive Views of Merely Instrumental Treatment

Although this is not a book focused on Kant, it will be clarifying to say more about the bearing of the emerging theory of conduct on interpreting his humanity formula: "*Act so that you use humanity, as much in your own person as in the person of every other, always at the same time as an end and never merely as a means.*" Suppose one takes the notion of treating persons merely as a means to figure in this formula simply *contrastively*, as opposed to expressing a negative injunction that goes beyond the end-respecting directive.[6] One might grant my solely-merely distinction and still wonder why, for Kant, treating a person merely as a means is prima facie worse than treating a person solely as one *given* that this also implies failure to treat the person even in part as an end.

One answer is implicit in my explication of the (prima facie) moral reprehensibility of the conduct constituted by merely instrumental treatment, as distinct both from

6. See Immanuel Kant, *Groundwork of the Metaphysics of Morals*, trans. Allen W. Wood (New Haven, CT: Yale University Press, 2002), 4:429, 46–47. Mary Gregor's translation also uses 'merely' (Cambridge: Cambridge University Press, 1997), 38. H. J. Paton uses 'simply' in translating the formula, but uses 'merely' in several places where the same idea is apparently expressed, e.g., secs. 428 and 429 (op. cit., 95 and 97). For a detailed informative discussion of the categorical imperative, and of Kantian ethics, see Allen W. Wood, *Kantian Ethics* (Cambridge: Cambridge University Press, 2008).

the possibly unobjectionable conduct constituted by many instances of solely instrumental treatment and from the act-type the agent instantiates in treating someone merely as a means. If Kant's notion of merely instrumental treatment of persons is even close to the notion I have explicated, then his prohibition of treating persons merely as means substantively adds to his injunction to treat persons as ends. My account of merely instrumental treatment supports the prohibition of it that he so resoundingly affirms. He repeatedly stressed that persons are ends in themselves and not mere means; and treating them merely as means, as we have seen, not only fails to treat them as ends but also bespeaks a disposition *not* to treat them as more than means. It is (on both his view and mine) a reprehensible behavioral indication of a tendency to undervalue or even deny their moral status. It fails to express respect for the other as a person, even if it need not rise to being in some way disrespectful.[7]

Although an interpretive analysis of even Kant's *Groundwork* is impossible here, it is appropriate to note one of the points that suggest that he took merely instrumental treatment to be morally objectionable in ways solely instrumental treatment is not. In the *Groundwork* Kant gives different kinds of accounts of violations of different duties. He appears to imply (in some places) that making a lying promise is wrong in part because it wrongfully uses someone merely instrumentally (at least on his understanding of that notion), whereas not developing one's talents and not doing good deeds for somebody one could readily help are

7. The kind of respect in question does not imply a standing positive evaluation; it is a matter of a kind of recognition of the moral status of the person(s) in question. For extensive discussion of the notion of respect see Darwall, op. cit.

not wrong in this way, but *do* constitute a failure to treat a person as an end.[8]

It is true that the value of persons, which in the context of discussing the humanity formula (the "intrinsic end" version of the categorical imperative), Kant suggests is the ground of the categorical imperative, might *also* at least partly underlie the wrongness of merely instrumental conduct. But it does not follow that the negative injunction to avoid such conduct does not significantly add to the force of the positive injunction to treat people as ends. Merely instrumental treatment of persons might be conceived as a way of *devaluing* them. By contrast, our not treating them as ends, even when culpable, may indicate only failure to respect their value. This is especially so where we ignore them when we should not (and in this way fail to treat them as ends) or when we treat them solely, even though not merely, as means, where we should treat them at least in part as ends.

In using the notions of merely instrumental and end-regarding treatment in the moral appraisal of behavior, much depends on how treatment is understood. If just any social interaction implies one person's treating another in some way, then there is a way I treat an usher from whom, as the performance is beginning, I hurriedly take a program held out for me in the half light and proceed to my seat.

8. In sec. 430, e.g., after Kant stresses how making a lying promise treats the promisee merely as a means (but does not mention at that point the implicit failure to treat the person as an end), Kant goes on to distinguish, in connection with duties to oneself, between what does not conflict "with humanity in our own person as an end" and what *harmonizes* with this end (p. 97 in Paton's trans.). It accords with his view also to distinguish, as I do, between what is not just inconsistent with this end—say, ignoring somebody one could, with little effort, help—and what is in *opposition* to it, such as callously manipulating the person to do one a service.

If I am fully preoccupied with avoiding disturbance of others, this behavior is likely not end-regarding treatment, but surely we need not take the action to be wrong. It is instrumental, but it certainly need not be treating the usher merely as a means. Is it even properly considered "treatment" at all? If so, one might consider it a minor wrong—failure to treat the usher as an end. Suppose one nonetheless *views* others as ends and so would be disposed to treat the usher as an end if, for instance, the usher summoned one to the rear to wait for the end of the first movement and this required some significant interaction. In that case, I think hurriedly taking the program from the usher is not wrong—if indeed it is a case of treatment at all, it is not one of treating the usher merely as a means. For reasons given in characterizing this notion in Chapter 1, I doubt that it is treatment (and have some doubt that Kant's overall view would commit him to construing it so).

It is important to distinguish what motivates a particular action toward another from the agent's overall motivational make-up at the time of action. Failure to view others as ends is (as Kant apparently maintained) morally criticizable in "normal" adults; so is lacking the kind of overall motivational make-up that disposes one to treat them as ends, should the situation call for it. But not all social interaction with others rises to treatment of them; and, where it does, failure to treat them (at least in part) as ends owing to solely as opposed to merely, instrumental treatment of them may merit at most minor criticism. If my hurried use of the usher as a program dispenser is a case of solely instrumental treatment, it need not indicate either defective moral views or the absence of sound and sufficiently motivating moral standards.

Examples like that of taking the program from an usher's outstretched hand illustrate something else that should be made explicit. Just as failure to treat someone as an end does not imply merely instrumental treatment, treating a person in a way that avoids merely instrumental treatment does not imply the positive conduct exhibited by treating persons as ends. The former is achievable by treating the person solely, but not merely as a means. Simply not acting toward someone at all is, of course, another way to avoid merely instrumental treatment, but it may not be creditworthy and would be criticizable where the situation calls for end-regarding treatment. Nor is end-regarding treatment entailed by simply doing good deeds for others, regardless of motive. Recall the case of rescuing someone from a fire only to interrogate and torture the person later. Very different trees can grow from the same soil.

III. Persons as Ends versus Good Ends for Persons

It may now be apparent that there is no act-type—no behaviorially specifiable type of deed—whose instantiation in conduct can constitute treatment of a person but *cannot* be a vehicle of (and so partly constitute) treating someone merely as a means. This is partly explainable on the assumption that such treatment is a kind of conduct, of which act-type is only *one* dimension. Treatment, as a kind of conduct, must have a behavioral vehicle, but the kind of vehicle that can figure in treatment of persons is almost unlimitedly broad.[9] The

9. The term 'behavioral' must be taken broadly and should allow for bad conduct *in foro interno*. Suppose reforming criminals vow to stop plotting crimes. Might they not properly tell their psychiatrists they are ashamed of their past conduct—plotting crimes—in their nighttime imaginings? In any case, we can speak of how one conducts one's planning and can sometimes bring moral as well as intellectual standards to bear on it. If morality does not regulate our internal conduct, it cannot adequately regulate our external conduct.

point holds, moreover, no matter how good the act's consequences are. Still, could there be *ends* of action that are so good for someone that the person's being treated merely as a means to *them* is not being treated merely instrumentally? Might such teleological clarification of the notion of merely instrumental treatment succeed where behavioral and consequential specifications fail?

Treating a person as an end is not equivalent to doing a good thing for the person. No matter what good we want to bring about for someone, there are various ways to bring it about, some of which we (morally) should want to avoid. I must not make my students brilliant and happy by forced brain manipulation, even if that is the most efficient means. Imagine, however, a saint's saying, of painstaking work with the sick, "I do it all for God." If the deeds do in fact benefit them and they recognize this, how can they be treated merely as means even if the saint is ultimately concerned only to please God and is constrained only by what is instrumental to that lofty mission? To see how, recall the distinction between treating others solely as a means and treating them merely so. Suppose the saint's sole motive for the actions in question is to please God. This does not entail merely (as opposed to solely) instrumental treatment. The saint need not be disposed not to care about any non-instrumental aspect of the patients' treatment. Consider a patient deeply offended by some aspect of the treatment. This would motivate any true saint to seek an alternative way to please God. Then we might have treating someone solely, not merely, as a means. But suppose the saint considered only a highly specific mode of treatment divinely approved, say immersion in icy holy water. If a singleminded commitment to this treatment exclusively for the purpose of pleasing God created the requisite disposition not to be concerned with anything else regarding the patient—any instrumentally irrelevant elements—then

despite the lofty end of the conduct, and even if it benefited the patient, the saint still treats the patient merely as
a means.[10]

To be sure, the saint's theological conviction might be
mitigatory regarding the conduct that manifests treating a
patient merely as a means, such as ritualistically immersing
the person, against protest, in the icy water. But my point
concerns the concept of treating people merely as means, not
the moral gravity of so doing. That treating someone merely
as a means is prima facie wrong does not foreclose the kinds
or degree of possible mitigation. Such treatment might even
be plausibly considered beneficent, but beneficence—at least
of this kind—does not preclude merely instrumental treatment. Moreover, although acting with this kind of zeal might
be acting piously, even in a certain way conscientiously, it
would not be acting *morally*.

Does the principle that we should treat persons as ends
require that *all* our (morally permissible) actions toward
others, at least if they represent treatment, be at least partly
motivated by *end-regarding desires*, as we might call desires
for some aspect of the good of a person? This requirement
would be highly demanding and would imply that treating an usher *only* as a means to finding one's seat is prima
facie wrong. This would surely be a mistake. But suppose the
requirement is instead to *view* others as ends (in themselves)

10. Granted, a true saint might note that the Biblical command to love God is *separate* from the command to love one's
neighbor; the latter is not equivalent to a command to love
one's neighbor *in order to* please God—or serve any further end.
Moreover, if God is taken to be perfectly good, I doubt there is
a good theological case for the permissibility of treating people
merely as means provided the treatment is intended to serve God.
There *may* be a theological case against even treating others *solely*
as a means.

in all such cases.[11] Perhaps so viewing others is a desirable
constraint on our treatment of others, as opposed to a motivating element. We might regard holding the view (which
one might hope to bring about in oneself if one's moral education has not produced it) as expressing a cognitive constraint on good moral character, in the sense that anyone not
holding or at least committed to the view has a defect of character. Moreover, perhaps so viewing others entails *acquiring*
motivation in certain cases; but it does not entail *having* any
particular motivation in actions toward them, say toward the
usher finding one's seats, though it would commonly tend to
constrain such actions, at least insofar as agents tend to avoid
acting incongruously with their relevant beliefs. This background cognitive constraint—the *positive view constraint*—on
understanding the injunction to treat persons as ends in
all our actions toward them is psychologically more realistic than the stronger, motivational constraint requiring that
all treatment of others be end-regarding. But, as desirable
as it may be for us to meet the former constraint, doing so

11. The attitudinal constraint is suggested by Kant in,
e.g., his contention that "[E]very rational being ... must in all
his actions ... always be viewed *at the same time as an end*." See
Paton, op. cit., 95 (4: 428). Indeed, shortly after saying this,
Kant speaks as if treatment of persons that is not merely instrumental is sufficient for (minimal?) treatment as ends: "Rational
beings ... are called *persons* because their nature already marks
them out as ends in themselves—*that is*, as something which ought
not to be used merely as a means and consequently imposes ...
a limit on all arbitrary treatment of them" (op. cit., 96; 4:428,
second set of italics added). A further question is what range of
acts Kant had in mind in speaking of how we "treat" humanity.
His four famous examples suggest a focus on morally significant
act-types and their motivation. My account covers conduct more
comprehensively.

does not appear necessary for morally acceptable treatment of persons.

In any case, even when the end of an action is outstandingly good, nothing needed for plausibly interpreting the prohibition of treating persons merely instrumentally precludes applying 'merely as a means'. The good end could still be both external to the other's good, as is pleasing someone else, and of the wrong kind, as is simply advancing one's own selfish agenda. Treatment of a person that is subordinate to some good end *involving* the person does not entail treatment *of* the person as an end.

IV. Internal and External Goods for Persons

Consider one other route to arguing that there are good ends for persons that are of such strongly positive character that one cannot treat people merely as means to *them*. Imagine that, perhaps by neural enhancement without their consent, I treat people as means to their *own* happiness or to fulfillment of their considered life-goals. How could being thus motivated by a good internal to their lives be treating them merely as means?

Suppose I treat Tim in a way that is in fact a means to his happiness, but I do *not* aim at his happiness for its own sake. Suppose, too, that there is a further end of my action, such as making him a better companion for others—an external good for him—and that I am disposed not to be concerned with any non-instrumental aspects of my treatment, including such potential reactions as his reflective protest against my putting him through brain surgery that I assure him will harmlessly enhance his happiness. As with the saint doing good for others only to please God, this is a kind of mitigated but still merely instrumental treatment. Treating people merely as means is a morally significant *way* of relating to them; it is not a matter of the act-type we instantiate in treating them in that way, and it is consistent with our aiming—instrumentally—at a good (such as their happiness) internal to their lives.[12]

More generally, for an ethics of conduct, *how* we treat people and *why* we do it in the way we do are important whatever the end we seek. If, moreover, we aim exclusively at a good external to another, we do not treat the person as an end even if we achieve an internal good for the person in so doing. Doing something that is good *for* another person, then, does not entail good conduct *toward* that person. For treatment of a person as an end, motivation of the action is crucial, and having, as a purpose in acting, good for a person is essential. If, however, that good is only instrumentally sought, the conduct is not treating the person as an end and may be merely instrumental. To be sure, good consequences of what one does toward the person can certainly be morally important; but realizing them does not transform instrumental treatment into end-regarding treatment.

The breadth of the notion of treating persons merely as a means calls attention to something easily overlooked when one's focus is (as in this book) on individual conduct as the primary case of acting morally. The notion of merely instrumental treatment is also applicable to institutional and even national conduct. This point underscores its importance in moral appraisal. An institution (and I use the term broadly enough to include businesses and other organizations) can,

12. Granted, the end could be *specified* in terms of the kind of treatment, e.g. as serving your good in a *way* that treats you as an end. My point is roughly that no specification of good for the person that is independent of the notion of treating as an end yields a way to specify a further end such that merely instrumental treatment subordinate to that end cannot constitute treating someone merely as a means.

by certain kinds of corporate or representative acts, treat its members or constituents, and certainly outsiders, merely as means. One nation can do this to the people of another. This holds, at least, on the assumption that whether an institution or nation is engaging in merely instrumental treatment is consequential on whether certain crucial agents who determine their policy are doing so (in which case the account of merely instrumental treatment of individuals can be appropriately extended). With that understanding, we can also see how one institutional entity can treat another merely as means. Even if such institutional treatment requires more than conduct by individuals with certain roles in the one toward individuals in the other, this conduct is the most important single element.

It is less clear how the notion of end-regarding treatment might apply at the institutional level, though it appears to have some applications in such cases. An institution can, on the basis of what its leaders want and do, care about the good of its members or role players—or those of some other institutional entity, and it can act in a way fitting to that caring. It is true that the good of an institution is something over and above the good of those who are its members at any given time, but the good of members *overall* is a major consideration in determining what is good for an institution. Given how the good of individuals figures in that determination, the distinctions we have seen been internal and external goods may be applied to institutional cases. Part Two will explore end-regarding treatment in a way that will suggest how all this may be so.

———

The ethics of conduct that has so far taken shape contrasts with both rule ethics and virtue ethics, though it provides a comprehensive framework of moral appraisal that can be integrated with either kind of ethical position. But neither a focus just on appraising actions nor even a focus on appraising actions in relation to traits of character provides an adequate basis for according due regard to the moral importance of conduct. What we have seen is that treating persons merely as means is not ruled out—nor is treating them as ends entailed—by doing something with the aim of realizing a good thing for them. End-regarding treatment is also not entailed by doing something toward others that in fact realizes a good end for them, even one internal to their lives. Such action is consistent with treating them merely as means. Treating persons as ends requires a special kind of motivating regard for their good conceived at least in part internally, as a matter of how well their lives go from the perspective of their experience. Such treatment, though not necessarily under that or any similar description, is plausibly viewed as central in respect for persons, as is avoiding treating them merely as means. Even beneficence as a trait underlying one's conduct and conceived as a virtue is not enough to make that conduct a case of treating the object of that beneficence as an end. Just what is required for treating persons as ends is a complex matter, and the next chapter will outline an account of that notion.

PART II

THE ETHICS OF RESPECTING PERSONS

5

TREATING OTHERS AS ENDS
IN THEMSELVES

So far, our focus has been mainly on merely instrumental treatment: what it is, how much control we normally have over whether we engage in it or in conduct approaching it, what range of act-types can be its vehicles, how it differs from end-regarding treatment, and how its ethical importance is connected with its three-dimensional character as conduct. The quite various examples we have considered confirm that such conduct toward persons—treating them merely as means—is prima facie wrong. It need not, however, be morally objectionable on the basis of any action that is its vehicle; an instrumental action can be a good deed done with malicious intent. This is one reason why the negative ideal constituted by merely instrumental treatment reaches beyond the common prohibitions of wrongdoing. Moral responsibility also extends to the manner of our actions, and conduct is appraisable in that dimension as well as on the basis of the action and motivation that partly constitute it. A good deed, even if done with beneficent intent, can be done so insensitively that the agent's conduct is objectionable. As all this shows, merely instrumental treatment is to be avoided, and seeing what it is and why it is prima facie wrong reveals much about the negative side of morality.

Treating persons as ends, by contrast, is morally desirable. End-regarding conduct toward persons normally manifests—and is often required by—a kind of respect for them. It should be uncontroversial that the notion of *merely* instrumental treatment is inapplicable to conduct in which one treats persons as ends, where the sense of 'end' is, roughly, 'something *for the sake of which* (or at least partly for the sake of which) one acts', not the more common sense in which ends can be brought about.[1] To some people it may seem that if there is a way that you treat me and it is not merely as a means, then it is also at least in part as an end. But this does not follow: you might be treating me *solely* as a means, which does not entail caring about me for my own sake. A purely negative account of treating a person as an end is fruitless.

How should we understand the positive notion, treating as an end? Given Kant's importance in making this notion prominent, some philosophers would naturally begin with his position, for instance by connecting such treatment with respect for others' autonomy. Let me reiterate that—important though it is—the difficult task of Kantian interpretation cannot be undertaken here. My aim is to provide an account that does not depend on, and may indeed help to clarify (and, very likely, refine), Kantian and other ethical theories. Let us first consider various kinds of treatment of persons in which it is plausible to take them to be ends of action, in the sense of that phrase in which it implies that an end the agent aims to realize by the action(s) in question is an aspect of their good.

1. Alan Donagan noticed this point about ends and explicated the Kantian notion compatibly with my account of treating persons as ends. See "Common Morality and Kant's Enlightenment Project," in *Reflections on Philosophy and Religion*, ed. Anthony Perovich, Jr. (Oxford: Oxford University Press, 1999), 139–156.

I. Caring about the Good of Others

Treating someone as an end in the sense just indicated surely embodies *caring*. More specifically, it entails treating the person in a way that is governed, and to some extent motivated, by caring about the good of the person (1) for its own sake (hence non-instrumentally) *and* (2) under some objectively satisfactory description of that good. The caring may be dispassionate. It may also be empathic or even loving. As our examples will bring out, a great variety of intrinsic motivational states may serve. Four further points are important here.

First, since treating a person as an end is governed by such intrinsic caring about their good, it cannot be merely instrumental. This holds even for treating a person partly as an end and partly instrumentally. Positively, end-regarding treatment implies some measure of *altruism*. That, as we saw with the saint manqué, is not entailed even by a high degree of beneficence, understood as entailing a readily realized tendency to do good deeds for others. Take a different example. Certain kinds of parents could treat their child beneficently, yet merely as a means to their own satisfaction. This need never show in their actions if there is never a disparity between their achieving their self-regarding ends and their doing things good for the child. By contrast, altruistic parents are motivated to do what is good for their children for the *children's* sake. Granted, beneficent conduct is normally to some degree altruistic; but conduct that is good for someone who is its object may, unlike altruistic conduct, still be a case of merely instrumental treatment.

Second, as these points indicate, we should distinguish between beneficence and *benevolence*. Benevolence—in the usual, largely social sense—is a matter of good will; beneficence is a matter mainly of good *deeds*. Good deeds need not manifest good will. A physician could painstakingly save a patient from bleeding to death wholly for the purpose of later extorting money. The action is beneficent, even if, in character, the *agent* is neither beneficent—having no tendency to do good deeds toward others—nor benevolent (though an agent could combine a degree of beneficence with such an ulterior purpose). To be sure, some degree of altruism is expectable given a high degree of beneficence or, especially, of benevolence, but there is no entailment: these three elements are mutually befitting, yet still quite distinct.

The third point here is that although the kind of description in question—under which the agent cares about the good of the other for its own sake—must be objectively satisfactory in a way that goes with the idea of treating a person as an end, the description need not be normative in content. Consider something done to eliminate pain, worry, or a threat of death. These notions are not intrinsically normative, though their application implies a normative description. Here the implied good is relief from the (descriptively) specified bad thing, such as pain.

In one way, relieving someone's pain is a potentially misleading example. It is something usually done mainly for the sake of the person in pain, so that the person is clearly treated as an end. But there are certainly exceptions. One can relieve an athlete's pain just to enable re-entry to the game. But consider asking someone to join one for lunch, where companionship is wanted. Or, take doing a job with others in the normal cooperative way. Here we treat the others as ends if we care about their good enough and in the right way—a way soon to be clarified further. It would be unusual, however, to do these things *only* for the other's sake and not partly for ours or partly to bring about their doing something further. Much of our treatment of others is justifiably mixed, in the sense that we appropriately care about their good but also treat them instrumentally to the extent required by the interaction or joint activity at hand or by the kind of relationship we have.

The pure cases of treating someone as an end are apparently not uncommon, though perhaps it is common for normal persons to come less close to them than they should. By contrast, one would hope that the pure cases of treating someone merely as a means are at best rare, and that approaching them is usually resisted. It is common in philosophical discussions of Kantian ethics to use the unqualified expressions 'treating as an end' and 'treating merely as a means' without bearing in mind the special character of the pure cases. This is often appropriate for end-regarding treatment, since even if we are doing something only in part for the good of someone else, we are very likely treating the person *partly as an end*. But although we can treat someone partly as an end and partly as a means, there are no degrees of merely instrumental treatment. Treating someone *merely* as a means excludes treating the person as an end *at all*. This is partly why it represents a kind of negative ideal.

The fourth point needed here concerns a question suggested by the case (in chapter 1) of caring about an elegant carving knife for its own sake. Can *anything* treatable merely as a means also be treated as an end? This is doubtful. Recall the case of the foul-tasting pill that is merely one of many and not worth searching for when lost in the grass. The notion of treating as an end is at least normally subject to a presupposition that it applies only to entities having interests or intrinsic value or at least non-instrumental importance. Perhaps the lost pill could qualify here, but we should not assume that just any possible object of merely instrumental treatment can do so. One thing that surely does qualify is the human body. A case in point is that of a woman who, though brain dead, was kept on a respirator for the sake of her unborn fetus, as the hospital considered necessary under Texas law. Her body was used instrumentally and, in the eyes of the protesting husband who claimed to know her wishes for such a case, might have been thought to be used merely as a means to sustain the fetus: the suit speaks of "mutilating, disturbing and damaging Marlise's deceased body."[2] The case illustrates that a human body can be treated merely as a means and suggests (without entailing) that someone can reflectively regard avoiding this treatment as taking priority over failing to treat a fetus as an end.

II. Two Kinds of Normativity

At this point we can better understand treatment of persons—end-regarding as well as merely instrumental—if we note a distinction I observe throughout (and take to be available to, even if not explicitly drawn by, other moral theorists). The distinction is between a notion's being moral in *upshot* and its being moral in *content* (which could also be called being moral in constitution). If, for instance, treating someone merely as a means clearly and a priori entails conduct that is prima facie wrong, the notion is moral in upshot. But neither its content nor the basic criteria for its application are moral; all of them may be (non-normatively) "descriptive"—a point important in understanding the role of the notion of merely instrumental treatment in moral discourse and appraisal. These points need development.

To see the distinction in relation to a concept that is highly significant in determining the kind of treatment constituted by conduct toward another person, consider

2. For a brief description of the case of Marlise Muñoz, see "Brain-Dead and Pregnant in Texas," *The Economist* 410, 8871 (January 25, 2014), p. 25.

the concept of pain. Taken generically, the notion is psychological: pain is (as a matter of conceptual truth) a psychological phenomenon normally having behavioral as well as introspectable aspects. Someone can understand the notion and identify the phenomenon without even having, much less applying, any moral concept. Yet pain also cries out for a palliative response: it makes such a response—and indeed end-regarding treatment—fitting, and it often both fully justifies that kind of response and highlights the fittingness of end-regarding treatment. On this second count, as a clear and a priori contributor to justification for palliative acts, pain is moral, hence normative, in upshot.

This reason-providing power of pain gives it great normative significance—enough to make it quite appropriate to speak of something's being moral (or normative) in upshot as a kind of normativity. This is particularly appropriate where, as with pain, the reason-providing element is plausibly taken to be self-evident.[3] But, in content, the concept is not deontic or axiological; nor is it normative in any other contentual respect: its normativity is not internal to the content of the concept but a consequence of its application. The concept is psychological and descriptive; but because the fact that some being is in pain clearly provides—and a priori entails—a reason (however slight) to do something to eliminate it, it bears an important relation to the normative "proper"—to what is normative in

3. This is how Ross took the grounds of the duties he considered crucial for understanding moral obligation. In *The Good in the Right,* esp. ch. 2, I have defended a revised version of this view and clarified the sense of 'self-evidence' in question. I believe that the clear a priori entailment crucial for the notion of normative upshot is also a case of self-evidence, but there is no need to argue for that here.

constitution. Pain has a normative upshot, though not a normative nature.[4] Pain is not moral or otherwise normative in constitution, though it is partly constitutive of what *is* moral in constitution. If no one could suffer pain, morality would be quite different from what it is.

Another way to see that the notion of treating a person merely as a means is not moral in content is to reflect on how singling out such treatment is among the ways we teach moral notions in the first place, rather as we point to injury and lying as examples of what constitutes wrongdoing. It does not follow from their having this kind of constitutive status, and it is not true, that the notions of injury and lying are moral in content or even non-descriptive. It is, to be sure, at least usually harder to *point to* treating merely as a means than to injury or lying, but children, at least, are sometimes transparently and cruelly manipulative in a way that strongly suggests an underlying callousness. "You sent your little cousin out in the cold rain to get you candy, and you didn't care what happened to her! You just used her."[5] This

4. Compare T. M. Scanlon's "buck-passing view." This view presupposes the distinction I am making, though making the distinction does not commit one to the view. (It does not presuppose—as perhaps my distinction need not—the apriority of the relation between what is normative in upshot and the reason it grounds, but taking this relation to be empirical is less plausible.) That elements normative in upshot (or propositions reporting them) are reasons, or at least reason-providing, does not imply that nothing else is, including normative facts such as that I have obligations to my friends. See his *What We Owe to Each Other* (Cambridge, MA: Harvard University Press, 1998), esp. 95–100.

5. Here one can quite literally point to the kind of behavior that manifests merely instrumental treatment, though the concept of such treatment is of course not an "observation concept" such

can both apply to very young children and be understood by them. And as they mature, children, like adults, can *feel* their being treated merely as a means in roughly the sense I have sketched, whether or not these terms are employed in describing the treatment.

These points do not require denying that moral and other normative concepts are common in the content of the motivation of agents treating others as ends. We can treat others as ends when we self-consciously act in order to promote their virtue or their good, so conceived. Parents often see themselves as wanting and doing things for the good, including the moral education, of their children. There will, however, be some further description applicable to their aim, such as 'teaching interpretive reading'. Even if the acts in question may be both conceptualized and motivating under descriptions like 'doing a good thing for my child', they are typically identifiable without epistemic dependence on moral or other normative notions. The notion of treating persons as ends, then, is like that of treating them merely as means in being applicable on a descriptive basis. They are also similar in being both higher-level (implying a lower-level act that is the vehicle of the treatment) and triple-barreled (requiring, in addition to a vehicle, a certain kind of motivation and having a definite manner even if not of a specific kind).[6]

as that of color and (certain) shape concepts. I take pointing in the relevant sense to go with a broadly ostensive way of *indicating* something and with the kind of perceptibility discussed in detail in *Moral Perception,* esp. chs. 1–3.

6. Kant may have sometimes viewed these notions not only as not specifically moral but also as not specifically normative. One reason to think this is his taking the humanity formula as equivalent to the universalizability formulas and explicating the latter in terms of "contradiction" and volitional impossibility tests. He also

III. Descriptive Grounds
of End-Regarding Treatment

Let us suppose that the notion of treating as an end may be viewed as normative in still another way: in the weak sense that there are objective constraints on its application that derive from good-making and bad-making features of the conduct in question. This might be seen as a kind of *normativity in application,* and it is in no tension with being normative in upshot or with the existence of "descriptive" sufficient conditions for the application of the notion. On certain assumptions, there might also be conditions of the same kind that are necessary *and* sufficient for its application. Recall the core of the account of treating persons as ends. It is treating them in a way that is governed, and in part motivated, by caring about their good (1) for its own sake (hence non-instrumentally) *and* (2) under some objectively satisfactory description of that good. It is thus motivated (at least in part) by an intrinsic concern with some aspect of their good.[7]

Is the Notion of End-Regarding
Treatment Naturalistic?

If, as I suggest, the agent treating someone as an end need not conceive that person's good in terms of notions that are moral or even normative in *content*, might we naturalize the concept of end-regarding treatment, as we found we

seemed to want to avoid dependence on moral notions in explicating even the humanity version of the imperative.

7. The notion of treating someone *purely* as an end requires that the treatment be motivated wholly by the relevant concern, but the broader notion is more appropriate to the point in the text.

could apparently do with that of merely instrumental treatment? The question is important in part because knowledge of the relevant non-moral properties seems more readily achievable than knowledge of moral properties or of many other normative properties; and even if it were not more readily achievable, knowledge of these non-moral properties would still provide a welcome distinct route to the knowledge of moral phenomena. Correspondingly, such non-moral, naturalistic knowledge would provide, for ethical theory, a partial defence of objectivity in ethics, and, for moral practice, a resource in dealing with disagreement in moral matters.

With this question of naturalization in mind, suppose that the good of persons can be hedonically or otherwise specified in terms of natural properties. One could then substitute in clause (2), which specifies the purposive range of end-regarding treatment, a disjunctive list of the relevant goods, *non*-normatively identified. For instance, we might say that end-regarding treatment is the kind of treatment that aims at *either* relieving suffering or providing pleasure or enhancing knowledge or easing the way to rewarding social relations, and so forth until all the goods for persons are specified. Agents treating someone as an end need not, of course, envisage the whole list, a perhaps very long disjunction. They need only be non-instrumentally motivated by a concern to realize one or more of the elements (such as pain reduction) in the other person. This is implicit in the point that the "descriptively" specifiable sufficient conditions for contributing to someone's good provide the notion of treating persons as ends with naturalistic *grounds*. Whether or not (true) moral judgments are expressions of natural facts and in that sense *equivalent* to descriptive judgments, their truth is consequential on, and hence ontically dependent on, such facts—the grounding facts, such as pain reduction, that we have been concerned with. Moreover, related to this ontic dependence of the notion of such treatment, our moral knowledge epistemically depends on such descriptive facts. Our knowing, for instance, that one person wronged another depends on our knowing such things as that the first seized the briefcase of the second.

The availability of naturalistically specifiable grounds of (prima facie) right and wrong actions is significant; they yield multiple paths from certain descriptive notions to the notion of the inherent moral character of actions. Suppose the sole motive for a deed is to keep one's promise to assist someone; there is then a path from this right-making descriptive ground to an element of moral worth in the action promised—which of course will not be merely instrumental. Knowledge-yielding paths of this kind are, moreover, often reliable as to the kind of treatment an agent's conduct represents, in the sense that the applicability to someone of a description such as 'laboring for hours in order to help a friend paint a house' makes it quite probable that we may truly ascribe treating the person at least partly as an end. Or, think of a mother nursing and softly singing to her baby. This description makes it highly probable that she is treating the child as an end.

The point that certain natural facts provide a path to moral knowledge goes beyond regarding (as do many ethical theorists) normative properties as consequential (hence supervenient) on natural ones. The descriptive notions in question, say that of relieving pain, are such that an understanding of the relevant normative concepts—above all, that of the good of a person—entails having a sense of what some of these sufficient conditions for contributing to that good are. These "descriptive" notions provide much of the material needed for an analysis of end-regarding treatment, even if—as I leave open—a full analysis requires appeal to the concept of the person's good.[8] The notions are not, however, simply *behavioral,* in the most natural sense of that term: we cannot specify any particular act-type such that every intentional tokening of that type must be end-regarding. Act-type is one thing; motivation is quite another. For any given type of action, more than one motive can serve as its basis, and at least commonly, more than one set of aligned motives may also constitute its motivation. Act-type does not dictate either the content of motivation or the number or strength of motivational elements. Taking account of these facts is essential for an adequate theory of the moral appraisal of persons and their behavior.

8. As suggested in the text, if we had a complete list of the things constituting a person's good, we might say that to treat a person (wholly) as an end is equivalent to doing something motivated entirely by the (non-instrumental) aim of realizing one (or more) of these goods for the person. Depending on the character of the list, we might consider this a (disjunctive) analysis. But some would insist on some unifying element, such as the notion of a person's good, and go on to argue that such an element must be a normative notion. Such normative unification is desirable, but neither the explication of a concept (like mine here) nor an account that guides its application requires a full-dress analysis of the kind in question. Neither does an account that specifies something different but also informative: a constitution relation. For a wide-ranging treatment of goodness that supports my approach to it, see Georg Henrik von Wright, *The Varieties of Goodness* (London: Routledge and Kegan Paul, 1963), e.g. his discussion of welfare—"the good of a being" (88)—in relation to ends, means, and happiness (86–112). For a case against taking the kind of disjunction in question to express a *property* (quite apart from whether it provides an analysis), see Paul Audi, "How to Rule out Disjunctive Properties," *Nous* 17, 4 (2013), 748–766.

The Element of Objective Success
in End-Regarding Treatment

One further matter must be considered in this section. I have so far left open whether treating someone as an end must be objectively (if minimally) successful in achieving the relevant good. It is natural to think that without success in an action toward someone we would have at best only *trying* to treat the person as an end. But what of surgeons who have excellent evidence that their operation will save the patient and do it by the highest standards prevailing at the time, yet lose the patient? Might they not still be treating their patients as ends? I find it plausibleto say so, but the attribution may be misunderstood unless a number of points are borne in mind.

First, suppose, as I hold, that the requirement to *realize* the good, or some good, sought in treating someone as an end is an objective success condition implying some positive result. A positive result, such as proper preparation of a patient for surgery, may be possible even if some good, or some aspect of the surgical good, that the agent competently aims at in the treatment is not realized. Properly—and caringly—preparing the patient and, beyond that, competently doing what the type of surgery calls for, are possible even if the operation fails to save the patient. Such preparation and surgical work are each one kind of end-regarding treatment. But what about the failed surgery? This brings us to a second point. The success requirement on a specific case of treating someone as an end—say, saving the person's life—may be quite different from the content requirement on the agent's motivation in such treatment: that it be aimed non-instrumentally at the other's good under some objectively satisfactory description. The surgeon fulfills the second requirement but not the first. If we distinguish the preparatory treatment from the later competent surgical treatment and the latter from the surgical outcome, we might say that whereas the first case is a success, the second, viewed in an overall way, is one of *trying* to treat the patient as an end and excusably failing. Given the complexity of surgery, however, it is misleading to describe it as an instance of a single case of treatment, whether instrumental or end-regarding.

The surgery case, then, shows a third point. Where treatment of someone occurs over time and through a complex of actions each of which—like washing, anesthetizing, and sewing a surgical wound—is a vehicle of a kind of treatment, there may be more than one treatment-type in question, and the overall, *compound treatment* may be constituted by a combination of successes and failed attempts. This is common with complex kinds of treatment. Just as a single segment of behavior can instantiate many act-types, a given case of extended treatment can instantiate many treatment-types and thus conduct types. We may then speak of either an integrated group of treatments as a partial success in treating the person in question as an end or of each instance of attempted end-regarding treatment—depending on the details—as a success or as an attempt that, perhaps quite excusably, fails.

To see a fourth point important here, suppose we did conceive treating someone as an end as possible when *no* good the agent aims at in the treatment is realized. We might still require that in these cases the agent must have objectively good justification for *taking* the action(s) partly constituting the treatment to suffice for realizing some good for the other. We might then say that where the agent has a belief to this effect but *lacks* good justification, we have a case of only trying to treat as an end. Given the possibility of this interpretation, one might wonder why, in this or some similar way, we should not view treating persons as ends more broadly and less objectively. Perhaps one might do so without doing violence to the concept. It seems more plausible, however, to take *some* kind of success as necessary for end-regarding

treatment and to recognize mitigation and excuse where the
agent is justified but mistaken in one or more crucial beliefs
about how to realize the good end governing the treatment.

Whatever one's view on the objectivity question, it is
important to see that trying to treat someone as an end
can be creditworthy treatment even if it fails. Nonetheless,
end-regarding treatment is better understood as a positive goal of conduct if it is taken to entail achieving some
positive result at which it aims. If, however, one should want
to conceive end-regarding treatment less objectively, one
might still arrive at essentially the same moral appraisals
of persons. A plausible, evidentially constrained subjectivist
account might, for instance, credit subjectively justified failure (say, to save a patient), as having the same moral worth
that my objectivist view would accord to conduct that, in the
right way, *excusably* fails to be end-regarding treatment but
is a creditworthy attempt at it. One view—*the epistemic view*
of end-regarding treatment—grounds end-regarding treatment in justified if ill-fated attempts and treats failure as a
liability of such treatment in an uncertain world; the other
view grounds end-regarding treatment in a kind of success,
but may morally credit agents' excusable failures to the same
degree as would the epistemic view. As the surgery case illustrates, the practical difference between the views is minimal.
The two will normally yield the same moral judgments in the
common cases in which the treatment is guided by justified
beliefs about what will contribute to someone's good.

If it is true that morality calls on us to treat others as
ends, we should expect that such conduct is aimed, non-
instrumentally, at least in part at their good. I have argued
that the good of persons, as properly understood here, cannot be defined in terms of what the agent takes it to be.
It is best understood in a broadly objective way in which

reducing suffering and enhancing enjoyment are prominently included among the criteria for enhancing a person's good. These notions are descriptive in an important sense, though also normative in upshot. As descriptive, they can play a role in understanding end-regarding treatment objectively and, to that extent, in objectively grounding moral standards; as normative in upshot, they enable us to single out some reasons for actions as good reasons. The next chapter will develop these ideas in ways that clarify end-regarding treatment and its role in moral thinking.

6

END-REGARDING TREATMENT
AND RESPECT FOR PERSONS

If the good of persons is objectively characterizable—even if partly in terms of their subjective states of, say, pain and pleasure—a perennial question must be explored further than in earlier chapters. Does morality require us actually to honor and promote that objective good in our conduct or is it sufficient for us to *believe* (with adequate justification) that what we are aiming at for a person is (objectively) good for the person? The question is not, as with our surgery case, whether morality requires that we be correct in thinking that our action toward the person will achieve our end; it is whether morality requires that we be objectively right in believing that end to be good. A related question is whether treating persons as ends in the way morality apparently requires entails caring just about the good of persons in general or also about the good of the *particular* or persons who are objects of the treatment. Philosophers have long differed over these questions, and we should explore them in some detail.

I. Good Deeds, Good Reasons, and Good Conduct

If treating persons as ends is end-regarding in the partly motivational sense I have outlined, then it is plausible to think that a deed of *any* act-type, however good, can be done for the wrong kind of reason to count as the vehicle of treating someone as an end. Recall the superficially admirable rescue of people from fire. This can be done in order to torture them later. It is consistent with treating them merely as means to fulfilling a diabolical military order and so can be an element in that kind of morally objectionable conduct. The doing of the deed *for* that reason and *in* that deceptive way is wrongful; the deed itself, simply as an act-token of the type, rescuing, is not. Good deeds alone do not suffice for good conduct.

It is natural, to be sure, to take a heroic rescue to be the sort of thing that shows concern for the well-being of others. One might think that this kind of deed and the multifarious good things people do for others are cases of treating others as ends, regardless of motivation. This is not true, but it points to a truth. Although, in the absence of caring about the good of others for its own sake, the heroic rescue does not count as treating others as ends, it *is* a case of *treating them as if they are ends,* in the sense of 'ends' implying that they have value in themselves and so warrant our doing things for their sake.[1] Treating *as* an end entails a specific kind of motivation; treating someone *as if* an end does not. Once this distinction is seen, we can stipulate a weak use of 'treating a person as an end' that would not require caring. Its application would be a matter of intentionally treating people in ways one would expect of someone who cares about their good for its own sake. It would have the same range of prima facie indicators as the richer notion.

1. I use 'as if they are' to avoid the counterfactual implication of 'as if they were', though that is more standard with this kind of subjunctive. It is an interesting question whether Kant, in some texts, had in mind some hypothetical notion of treating as an end.

We would have, then, two closely related construals of treating persons as ends, one motivational, the other not. On the first, the notion of treating as an end does not have behavioral sufficient conditions, and no act-type automatically qualifies; on the second, the notion does have behavioral sufficient conditions and is instantiated by the kinds of (intentional) deeds we would expect from a rational, properly informed person who actually treats others as ends in the motivational sense. If, however, there are behavioral sufficient conditions for treating someone as an end, then given that any (lower-level) act-type that represents treatment of a person can instantiate treating a person merely as a means, an act meriting this instrumental description could *also* satisfy the weaker, "good deed construal," of treating as an end. A good deed like rescuing people, even done with a view to torturing them later, could then be a case *both* of treating merely as a means and of treating as an end in the weak sense. Must we accept this odd consequence?

One response to this odd and perhaps paradoxical consequence is to say that the notion of treating merely as a means should be given a second, partially behavioral construal on which it is ruled out by the kind of good treatment illustrated by the rescue taken in itself. I do not find this view plausible. For one thing, neither the notion of *being* a means nor that of doing or using something *as* a means (for an instrumental reason) limits the eligible act-types in this way. Virtually anything can be a means, or be believed to be a means, to virtually anything else that can be brought about. Indeed, one good way to conceal treating people merely as a means would be to find a way of doing it that appears to be treating them as if they were ends. Second, as we have seen, there can be something quite reprehensible in an agent's doing even good deeds when so acting treats someone merely as a means in the sense I have explicated, which implies a disposition not to be concerned with anything that is not instrumentally relevant to the agent's end.

In the light of these points bearing on the attempt to conceive treating as an end either in terms of *trying* to achieve an objective good end or, behaviorally, in terms of *actually* achieving such an end (as by rescue from a fire), we should reject those conceptions. Neither well-aimed endeavors nor successful deeds abstracted from motivation are sufficient to guarantee end-regarding treatment. We should also reject another ostensibly simpler approach than the one I propose—a negative one. Just as we cannot understand treatment as an end, negatively—for instance, as treatment that is *not* merely instrumental—we cannot understand treatment merely as a means, negatively, say as failure to treat as an end. As Part I showed, conduct in which the agent fails to treat someone as an end need not be instrumental treatment *at all*. It may be simply negligent or disrespectful, as where, just for fun, someone detonates thunderous fireworks in a residential neighborhood at dawn. This is bad but not instrumental conduct.

Another tempting simplification in accounting for treatment as an end would require that the action that is its vehicle be intentional. Given how much of our conduct involves intentional action toward others, one might think that treatment of persons (and conduct generally) must be intentional, at least in the sense that any action constituting its vehicle is intentional. This depends on how the vehicle is determined. What if the conduct is hurting someone's feelings by making a speech indicating why some other candidate for an office is best? One can hurt feelings knowingly but not intentionally. Suppose I am obligated to make a plausible nomination speech, but, instead of stating uncontroversial facts that are well known to me and amply justify my nomination without offending or hurting the other candidate, I cite only good traits of my nominee that, though possessed by her, are the very ones in which the rival takes pride. The conduct is reprehensible; I am not at all tactful in what I say that might wound the other candidate, even though I do not mean to offend. Even if I like the other candidate and sincerely say so, my insensitivity is not consonant with the respect for the feelings of others that should go with treating them as ends.

The case illustrates something important: the scope of our moral responsibility for our actions goes beyond those performed intentionally. It extends to conduct foreseeably affecting someone toward whom one may not be doing anything, at least intentionally or even knowingly. Foreseeability of the effects of what we do and our actual or potential control of it, including avoidability of the action, are crucial, whether or not the action in question is intentional. We can of course make amends after the fact. But in most of our conduct, foresight is better than hindsight.

Indeed, my conduct in the nomination might simultaneously exhibit both treating one person, the lauded nominee, as an end, and failing to treat another, the bypassed offended alternative candidate, as an end, though without in any way treating that person as a means even if the treatment is, as undervaluing the candidate, bad. This is not paradoxical: given the complexity of conduct and the common possibility of conduct toward more than one person at the same time and through the same actions as vehicles, we should expect a single case of conduct (such as giving a nomination speech) sometimes to manifest different kinds of treatment toward different persons (possibly including both end-regarding and merely instrumental treatment).[2]

---

2. This point is best understood on the assumption that conduct-tokens are individuated coarsely (apart from their motivational constituents, which, as intentional, must be finely individuated). Thus, a single instance of conduct can bear different conduct-descriptions, such as 'treating the client merely as a means

In the insensitive nomination case, the main persuasive conduct does not involve intentionally hurting feelings; but the nominator's avoidable failure to prevent hurting the feelings of the alternative candidate is also both a failure to treat that person as an end and bad treatment. Doubtless *some* action that is central in the offensive conduct must be intentional, but it might not be the action specified in appraising that conduct, such as nominating Maria. The nomination speech, moreover, even if short, could also exhibit unfair treatment of a yet another person (wrongly overlooked) and instrumental manipulation of still another, whom the nomination forces to shift allegiance from the bypassed candidate to the nominated one.[3]

II. End-Regarding Treatment, Intention, and Interpersonal Behavior

The case of failing to treat someone as an end without intentionally doing anything wrong enables us to see something more. Consider speaking in stentorian tones in a crowded restaurant. The action of speaking can be a vehicle of bad treatment not only when it constitutes intentional wrongdoing but also without even being knowingly performed. This excessively loud speaking is bad conduct and also a bad way of treating others even if it is merely spontaneous ebullience and is not intentionally annoying or, *as* loudly speaking or

to profit' and 'treating the client merely as a means to financial benefit'. Both could be cases of treating one's employer partly as an end.

3. The nomination case illustrates how the account of conduct developed in this book may help to explain why, as Derek Parfit argues in *Does Anything Really Matter?* (forthcoming), an action need not be less seriously wrong because it is a foreseen but not intended result of what one is intentionally doing.

disturbing others, intentionally or even knowingly done. The *speaking* is intentional; its manner and immediate effect on others, which yield bad conduct in the situation, are not intentional and may be plainly unintentional. Yet the conduct might be a clear failure to treat others as ends.

The restaurant case nicely illustrates something else: that, however important motivation usually is in rendering conduct overall good or bad, conduct can be bad when its motive is unobjectionable. Here, the motive might be simply to get one's point across. The example also shows that an act-type which is the vehicle of the bad conduct—here, communicating one's point—may also be unobjectionable.[4] The three dimensions of conduct should be assessed in relation to one another, but they may also be appraised independently in the different categories to which they belong—act-type, motivation, and manner of performance.

The kind of bad treatment of others illustrated by the nomination and restaurant cases is not instrumental, and so, unlike treating them merely as means, is not criticizable as a wrongful way of using them. But it does constitute objectionably *failing* to treat others as ends. These cases also show, then, that even if the moral assessment of treatment of others does not require its being either instrumental *or* end-regarding, that treatment may still be morally appraised in relation to at least one of those notions. I reiterate that although merely instrumental treatment is like solely instrumental treatment in being motivated *only* instrumentally,

4. As noted earlier, one could argue that there is an objectionable act-type here, namely yelling or at any rate booming. I have already suggested that this strategy may conceal, but does not eliminate, the distinctive element of manner of action. Not only can booming, for instance, be instantiated in different ways; but the notion itself is implicitly compound—it is essentially speaking in a certain loud manner.

the former should be conceived partly in terms of the additional morally significant elements. This leaves open that solely instrumental conduct may be prima facie wrong in failing to be end-regarding; but it also leaves open that unlike merely instrumental conduct, it may be as unobjectionable as politely asking the time of day. It may be true that, in important matters, our conduct toward others should embody treating them at least partly as ends, but it does not follow that all treatment of others, however routine, must meet that standard.

If conduct need not have an intentional action as its vehicle, as with bad treatment constituted by speaking in stentorian tones, must it be interpersonal? One would think not, provided one can treat *oneself* wrongfully. This seems quite possible, for instance where people mutilate or degrade themselves. It is less clear whether conduct need be any kind of treatment of persons. Imagine a rebellious child of politically correct parents simply composing, in secret, ugly, racist, scurrilous verses for a kind of counter-cultural pleasure. This could be bad conduct even if it is not a way of treating oneself or anyone else and has only *potential* bad effects on anyone. Still, the conduct might at least verge on degrading oneself, and degrading any person is surely a kind of bad treatment. The badness might ethical as well as aesthetic, and a kind of moral guilt would not be inappropriate, at least in retrospect. Again, we can see the immensely wide scope of ethical standards and how they extend even to solitary conduct.

As wide as the notion of conduct is, the scope of ethical evaluation is wider still. It concerns how we affect others even if this is not by any kind of treatment of them. Affecting others is essentially causal in a way treatment of them need not be, and the former does not imply the latter. Removing shoes in anticipation of a security request might affect others (who follow suit), but is not a way of treating them or an instance of conduct toward them.[5] It might or might not be morally significant; it could be wasting crucial time where there is no such requirement, causing one's missing a plane and thereby an important deadline. Even that significance, however, might not raise the action to the level of treatment of a person. Similarly, someone's entering the room might distract me; this need not be treating me a certain way, though it *affects* me. To be sure, if I am conducting a class, it might be both treatment of me *and* morally significant. The interpersonal context in which an agent does something affects whether we have a case of treatment of another person or mere action in relation to someone else; if the former (though not only then), we have an instance of something for which the agent bears moral responsibility.

III. The Particularity of Persons and the Interchangeability of Means

A further requirement for treating persons as an end concerns what it is to be a particular person. It appears that in so treating others we must not regard them as simply instances

---

5. There are interesting borderline cases. Suppose that, by humming on a dark street, we surprise someone and thereby cause a heart attack. Is this treatment of the person? What *kind* of humming we do, in volume, tone, and melody, matters. If the humming is treatment, is it a kind that is prima facie wrong? Again, we can see that context matters. If, in the isolated darkness of the wee hours, it constitutes taking the other person by surprise, then it is potentially reprehensible conduct; if, in good light and a safe neighborhood, it would simply alert an acquaintance to the presence of some clearly unthreatening person, 'conduct' would seem too weighty a term. More will be said about conduct, and specifically about treatment, in the next chapter.

of a type of person. Suppose it is Sally I am treating as an end. Then my concern is not with just anyone who fits (as she might) the description 'the person who currently needs my assistance most'. And if I am talking to a friend in order to help with a problem, I should not be indifferent to an instantaneous substitution of someone just like my friend with all the right memory impressions and other mental characteristics. If, however, all that mattered were the end of talking to *a* friendly person with exactly the set of traits in question, indifference to substitution would not be inappropriate. If my concern is for *her*, then *her* understanding of what I say is part of my end, and my communication with her for its own sake is my purpose.

Cases like these bring out a basic contrast between ends and means. An end, at least where it is a person, may not be assumed to be, without loss of anything important, *interchangeable* with any end just like it,[6] whereas a means, as such, *is* thus interchangeable with any means instrumentally as good; and treating something (including a person) merely as a means at least normally embodies a disposition to consider it interchangeable with something instrumentally as good. Our attitudes and motivation regarding persons as ends are particular. If, in treating Sally in a certain way, I am concerned about her only as an instance of a kind of person, then I am treating her as a means, though not necessarily merely so. Enhancing her good can be included in my aim,

---

6. An end of action may be represented by an act-type (or other universal), e.g. giving her flowers. Here, unless I have particular flowers in mind, any act-token of the relevant type will do. Even if I have certain special flowers in mind, indefinitely many tokens of the act of giving them will fulfill my desire. But *they* are not interchangeable without loss of identity through time. If personal identity rather than qualitative similarity matters crucially in human relations, then persons are like flowers in this.

but not as *her* good: only as the good of a person who (let us say) will grow up to do fine paintings.

It must be granted, however, that our attitudes and motivation are in a certain way quite properly generalizable, given that the normative properties of actions or even of persons are consequential upon their descriptive natural properties (or in any case non-normative properties). Perhaps, for instance, communicating with your perfect duplicate is, in a purely qualitative sense, as good intrinsically as communicating with you. It does not follow that to treat a person as an end permits *considering* the person interchangeable with anyone qualitatively identical. Indeed, if I made a promise to *you*, then strictly speaking I have not kept it even if I carry out exactly the kind of deed promised toward your duplicate, and in the approving presence of that person, and where no one has the slightest inkling that a perfect duplicate has supplanted you. In this kind of case, at least, moral obligation is strictly particular. The obligation of beneficence is of course not necessarily so conceived; I can do as much good (at least non-moral good) by "fulfilling" the promise—*quasi-fulfilling* it, we might say—toward the duplicate as toward the promisee. Moreover, even where (unknowingly) I do not strictly fulfill my promise, in the imagined case I am excusable for not doing so.

Given the association between the topic of merely instrumental versus end-regarding treatment and Kantian ethics, it should be no surprise that the points made here (among others made in this book) bear on consequentialism, conceived as roughly the view that what we ought to do is maximize the good (different accounts of the good, of course, are used by different consequentialists, but it is usual for the view to take non-moral good as the basic kind). For a pure consequentialism—and I do not claim that any philosopher holds this view, even if some consequentialist pronouncements may imply it—we are all properly means to certain ends, say to optimizing the happiness of persons (for illustration I presuppose a possible version of Mill's utilitarianism). I therefore must treat myself and everyone else as a means to this end. Being a person capable of hedonic states, I matter as a potential contributor to this end, but only as such. If I thus may not treat myself *merely* as a means (though I may come asymptotically close to this), I may treat myself as an end only interchangeably with anyone else who would be made equally happy by (or would equally contribute to) the distribution of, for example, talents, funds, medical supplies, or other things that conduce to the good.

Suppose I have internalized consequentialism in such a way that I am motivated entirely by the desire to maximize (non-moral) intrinsic goodness in the lives of persons. I then have no motivation to treat anyone as an end in a sense precluding interchangeability. This is not to say that I may treat anyone *merely* as a means. Everyone's happiness matters. Hence, I must care about making others happy or unhappy, and such caring will dispose me to treat others as ends. Moreover, in a certain way I must be impartially good to persons. On *these* counts, consequentialism has implications for everyday conduct that significantly overlap those of a Kantian theory in which treating persons as ends is central. This very point is part of what explains why it can be difficult to see that a pure consequentialism makes no place for giving *independent* moral weight to treating particular persons as ends.

If (some) consequentialists must take the aggregate good of persons (or persons and other sentient beings) as the overarching end, it may seem to follow that they should acknowledge a prima facie obligation to treat persons as ends. Once interchangeability is fully understood, we can see an ambiguity here. If our concern is just to maximize (say) the happiness of persons, we may not be indifferent to personal happiness, i.e., the happiness of *persons in general;* but we also may not give special consideration to the happiness of any *persons in particular,* including ourselves and our families. Treating persons as ends, however, presupposes their particularity. Now in the world as we know it we cannot be duplicated. But suppose I could be painlessly and unknowingly dispatched in favor of, and as a means of making an appropriate place for, someone just like me except for far more capacity to be happy in the future (perhaps because of better future health owing to differences in body chemistry that are discernible only by sophisticated chemical tests). Shouldn't someone who is wholeheartedly committed to (say) happiness as the basic value governing human conduct (and would suffer no guilt) do the unnoticeable deed? Who else need even know it has been done? Here, then, is a case in which, although persons in general ("humanity") may not be treated merely as means, a particular person could be so treated—or at least treated in a way that approaches merely instrumental treatment—if the result should be sufficiently good for a person of the same type.[7]

Indeed, both end-regarding treatment and merely instrumental treatment, as I have been explicating them, are possible toward oneself. Might one not both fail to treat oneself as an end and approach treating oneself merely as a means? Think of a someone bereft of self-esteem who is committed to serving a demanding master. Such persons could

7. The treatment might only approach the merely instrumental because the agent's caring about the good of persons in general would tend to rule out indifference to all non-instrumental aspects of the substitution strategy. But the force of this constraint could approach zero where, say, suffering on the part of the original person is infinitesimal in relation to the good produced by the successor.

not only fail to treat themselves with appropriate intrinsic concern for their own good—if indeed they must have such concern—but could also treat themselves as means to satisfying their master and, in doing so, have a strong disposition not to be concerned with any non-instrumentally relevant aspects of the treatment.

Broadly speaking, what we are seeing is a contrast between two kinds of ethical position. One is an ethics in which treating persons as ends is, in much human interaction, a central prima facie obligation—as it is in the ethics of conduct outlined in this book—or (arguably) any ethics in which respect for persons as individuals is essential. The other is an ethics of consequences for the (non-morally defined) well-being of persons, which is an ethics in which respect for the *category* of persons is essential. There may be much agreement between the two approaches in the kinds of deeds we should do, but the overlap seems far from complete and there are major differences in the theories, normative reasons, and attitudes that go with each approach. This is not to suggest that the notion of respect for persons can be fully explicated in terms of treating them as ends. But such treatment seems necessary, even if it is not sufficient, for treating persons, as individuals, with respect.

An account of treating persons as ends and of avoiding treating them merely as means goes a good distance toward clarifying respect for persons, even if such an account is not strictly necessary for understanding respect for persons as individuals. By contrast, it appears that a pure consequentialism (one that, like hedonism, countenances only non-moral goods as basic types of good) cannot account for any more than a contingent obligation, not intrinsic to morality, to treat persons, *as* individuals, as ends. There would be no basic requirement to do this, since doing it might interfere with actions that are better for the aggregate good of persons. The overall point is that from the fact that persons in general may not be treated merely as means (say to the good of non-persons) and must be treated, in a *collective* way, as ends, it does not follow that every particular person must be treated in accordance with these standards. If that is so, then consequentialism, in many forms, at least,[8] provides only contingent protection of what intuitively seem to be moral rights, and it cannot fully account for respect for persons as individuals.

————

Treating someone merely as a means is instrumental in a way that requires affecting the person and is prima facie wrong. By contrast, treating someone as an end, in cases where it requires affecting the person, is, on many ethical views, prima facie obligatory at least where there is an obligation to engage in conduct toward the person in the first place. We have seen by implication much about what constitutes such treatment, since we have seen much about the nature of treatment of persons and various points about how a good deal of what appears to rise to it does not do so. It has become apparent, moreover, that where persons as such matter in the way they do in an ethics of conduct in which their treatment is central, a consequentialist ethical theory must at least be highly qualified to do justice, even at the level of overt behavior as opposed to that of conduct, to the moral standards implicit in an ethics of conduct. All this can be better seen when more is said about what constitutes treating persons as ends and how it is to be appraised. The remaining

8. There may be forms of rule-consequentialism that can plausibly be taken to avoid this result. See, e.g., Brad Hooker, *Ideal Code, Real World* (Oxford: Oxford University Press, 2000).

chapters largely concern such positive treatment. We begin, in the next chapter, with the role of the recipients' psychological make-up, especially in beliefs, attitudes, and desires, in determining whether conduct toward them is or is not treating them as ends.

7

AUTONOMY AND THE MORAL
SIGNIFICANCE OF OUR
SELF-CONCEPTIONS

It should now be evident that there are normative limitations on what constitutes treating a person as an end, whereas merely instrumental treatment is not subject to such limits: there is no normative standard it must meet, no nadir of evil to which it cannot sink, and no positive end so good that any treatment aimed at that good is thereby prevented from being merely instrumental. Even if those who burned women at the stake thought it would make them eternally happy, it is too cruel (among other things) to be treating them as ends.[1] Treating a person as an end implies both an intrinsic concern with the person's good and limited room for error about what constitutes it.

Might the normative limitations on end-regarding treatment vanish, however, if the person who receives it reflectively

1. I am assuming both error and unjustified belief on their part (this doesn't require denying the possibility of eternal happiness, but I assume burning them at the stake would not produce it). If their belief could be both justified and true, the case could be argued to be, like subjecting people to life-saving surgery, one of end-regarding treatment requiring the torture as an element. Much in this chapter bears on appraising the issue.

endorses the agent's erroneous conception of that person's good?[2] The issue here is nothing less than the degree of subjectivity that is incorporated in the constitution of personal goodness. The good of persons surely has an objective side; the pain of napalm burns is objectively bad, and delight in playing soccer or hearing a virtuoso string quartet playing Mozart is objectively good. A person's good is surely affected by such experiences. But does personal goodness also have a subjective element? And if it does, how important is that element in determining what constitutes treating persons as ends?

I. Psychological Dispositions and the Basis of Consent

Suppose a man believes himself possessed by a demon and asks to be burned alive. Must doing as he asks be treating him as an end? I think not. Even if he can rationalize his belief, that seems not to change the case except in raising the degree of mitigation for acceding to his request. Suppose, however, that he believes he must be sacrificed to pacify terrorists, where his belief is rational and he thinks that, as a realization of his ideals, this sacrifice is ultimately for his good. Might acceding, say by giving him a painless overdose of morphine, now be end-regarding?

There are borderline cases. Given some kinds of error on his part, such as clear falsehood in his belief that his

2. Here it may be useful to compare the role provided for reflective endorsement by Christine Korsgaard in *The Sources of Normativity* (Cambridge: Cambridge University Press, 1996). For a detailed critical treatment of her use of this notion in interpreting Kant, see Jens Timmermann, "Value without Regress: Kant's 'Formula of Humanity' Revisited," *European Journal of Philosophy* 14, 1 (2006), 69–93, and Parfit, op. cit., esp. 224–226. For a recent treatment of the Formula by Korsgaard, see "Valuing Our Humanity," forthcoming.

sacrifice would realize his ideals, one could still fail to treat him as an end even in doing as he asks. Given other kinds of error—the kinds not easily discoverable by even careful, informed reflection—perhaps there need be no such failure. Suppose, for instance, that although he is in error, determining this requires weeks of investigation. Perhaps in this case doing as he asks can be treating him as an end despite its objective failure to contribute to his good as understood (instrumentally) in terms of fulfilling his aim of preventing terrorism. If so, this may be because what is objectively good for a person is not *wholly* independent of what the person, in this highly rational and very reflective way, wants or would want. This point holds in part because our exercise of autonomy in reflectively choosing as we do is itself a good thing in our lives. To at least a significant degree, this is a good thing independently of *what* we choose; and others' fulfilling our desires is, in the abstract, a common element in their acting out of concern for our good, though the process itself may of course have results whose badness outweighs its value.

Here we should recall the distinction between internal and external goods for persons. Suppose that taking account of the exercise or of certain hypothetical exercises of a person's autonomy is a good that partly determines what it is to treat that person as an end. This *kind* of objective valuational constraint on end-regarding treatment of persons is a partly internal and a less objective requirement than, say, reducing the person's physical suffering. For one thing, taking account of autonomy would give some weight to certain kinds of self-regarding desires, including some that are not rational. But end-regarding treatment must still meet some external, objective constraints.[3] If (as I leave open) the notion of

3. This view is fruitfully compared with one suggested (even if not unqualifiedly) accepted by Kerstein, *How to Teat Persons:* "a person's action is autonomous if and only if she is acting on some

treating a person as an end would then have a normative element, say by essential reference to respecting *rational* desires of a certain kind, the more important point is that the notion could still be non-*moral*. Our application of it, then, need not presuppose any independent moral judgment.

One reason our conception of our own good is insufficient for determining what constitutes treating us as ends is that we are highly fallible concerning that good. Nonetheless, the content of our conception of our good can (when we are rational and adequately informed) determine one aspect of that good. Suppose that bringing about our good so conceived would, to our surprise, disappoint us, even pain us—which is certainly possible given our fallibility about what achieving our ends will be like. Nonetheless, if someone who knows this *overrides* such a conception, say by denying us the chance to pursue the realization of our good as we conceive it, this is a kind of denial of autonomy. Even if, for instance, we may sometimes discount the content of a confused or mistaken person's judgment, we may not act as if the person's *making* it and wanting to be treated accordingly does not matter. Suppose a friend depressed about a professional failure asks to borrow a shotgun we would normally lend on request, but we know that agreeing would lead to an insufficiently considered suicide. We may decline, but we

preference of hers and, based on reflection on her values, she either does, or, if she thought about it, would choose to have this preference even in the light of understanding how it arose in her" (p. 21). His note here cites, as providing "a more elaborate account along these lines," David DeGrazia, *Human Identity and Bioethics* (Cambridge: Cambridge University Press, 2009). It will be clear in what follows that, on my view, the problems undermining the normative authority of first-order psychological attitudes are not overcome by the subject's disposition to have higher-order preferences for them even guided by genetic information.

need a good reason. Even then, we would have a prima facie obligation to explain in due course why we declined.

A related point about our conception of our own good is that to treat people as ends (assuming they are competent adults), we must care about their *capacity* to see the action(s) in question as compatible with their good. This capacity is crucial for their autonomy, conceived roughly as self-government guided by certain standards.[4] The capacity, which I take to entail having a conception of one's good, is important for human dignity, essential to normal personhood in adults, and, in its normal manifestations in determining the shape of their lives, an aspect of their good.[5]

The point is not that if we treat others as ends they must *consent* or be disposed to consent, to what we do—which I take to be normally a matter of consent to the vehicle of the treatment, perhaps including its manner of performance (the consent view is not normally accompanied by consideration of possible consent to an agent's acting *for* a particular reason). To be sure, it is plausible to say that *if* the persons in question are sufficiently rational and adequately informed, they could (and perhaps likely would) consent. But even then, we cannot say that they definitely would do so, since (for one thing) aesthetic and personal preferences can block

4. I take autonomy to be more than mere control of oneself in serving whatever desires are regnant at the time. For an account and discussion of alternative conceptions of autonomy, see my "Autonomy, Reason, and Desire," *Pacific Philosophical Quarterly* 72, 4 (1992), 247–271 (reprinted in my *Moral Knowledge and Ethical Character* (Oxford: Oxford University Press, 1997).

5. As to children, non-competent adults, and animals, their interests must be taken into account in some hypothetical way. We can imagine how a child would see something as compatible with its good, and we can frame a notion of the good of animals incapable of a conception of their own good.

consent even where no "objective" harm would be done by the act in question. As the normative significance of such personal preference indicates, rationality may sanction a wide range of preferences without requiring the satisfaction of any particular one of them; and treating persons as ends entails giving weight to their choices among such discretionary options—even to some of their whimsical choices. My main point here is that treating persons as ends requires caring (at least in an implicit way) about whether they have a *basis* for consent and (regarding rational persons) about what they would or would not consent to on a suitable basis. I need not have beliefs specifically about what constitutes their basis for consent; but my dispositions must be such that how others do or would regard what I do toward them matters to me.

End-Regarding Treatment as Conceived
in Kant's *Groundwork*

Did Kant think otherwise? One might suppose that "According to Kant, you treat someone as a mere means whenever you treat him in a way to which he could not possibly consent."[6] Given the breadth of this description, its application does not require instrumental treatment (as Kant apparently intends

6. See Christine M. Korsgaard, "The Reasons We Can Share: An Attack on the Distinction between Agent-Relative and Agent-Neutral Values," in Ellen Frankel Paul, Jeffrey Paul, and Fred D. Miller, eds., *Altruism* (Cambridge: Cambridge University Press, 1993), 45. Cf. *"[V]ery* roughly speaking, you are not treating him merely as a means if he consents to what you are doing" (op. cit., 46). (I assume Korsgaard is using 'as a *mere* means' and '*merely* as a means' interchangeably.) As indicated above, I view even reflective consent to a kind of treatment as too weak a condition to guarantee that the treatment is end-regarding, though some of what Korsgaard says plausibly strengthens the suggested condition; e.g., "To treat someone as an end is . . . to respect his

to require). There are likely many kinds of treatment that are not instrumental at all but to which certain rational persons could not consent. These include repugnant modes of medical treatment that are simply matters of surgical or therapeutic style and not the agent's means to anything. Consider, too, insensitive collateral treatment of us such as damaging military maneuvers on our property, where the damage done to virgin forest is not intended or a means to the perpetrators' ends but merely foreseen by them.

Kant does, however, appeal to something like hypothetical consent, in clarifying the humanity formula: "the man whom I seek to use for my own purposes by such a [lying] promise cannot possibly agree with my way of behaving toward him, and so cannot share the end of the action."[7] This suggests that the ability, on the part of the recipient of

right to use his own reason to determine whether and how he will contribute to what happens" (46). Cf. Onora O'Neill: "We use others as *mere means* if what we do reflects some maxim *to which they could not in principle consent.*" See "Ending World Hunger," in Tom Regan, ed., *Matters of Life and Death*, 3rd ed. (New York: McGraw, Hill, 1993), reprinted in Louis P. Pojman, ed., *Ethical Theory*, 4th ed. (Belmont, CA: Wadsworth, 2002), 286; and "To treat others as ends in themselves we must . . . treat them as rational autonomous beings with their own maxims" (p. 287 in Pojman). Depending on our account of *why* a person could not consent, the former characterization might be only wider, but not narrower, than mine; but it differs greatly in requiring (as arguably Kant did) the complex idea that merely instrumental treatment must be understood in terms of somehow reflecting a maxim. The second characterization might bear a reading that brings it close to mine—apart from apparent inapplicability to non-rational beings, who cannot have maxims.

7. *Groundwork*, sec. 429, 97 in Paton. Note that Kant apparently does not treat "way of behaving" as indicating just act-type, and in this case my notion of conduct might serve in the context.

treatment, to share the agent's end(s) is crucial. But that ability might diverge from the ability to give rational consent. A masochist could share at least some ends of a sadist who wants to cause pain; but here consenting need not be rational and might not legitimate sadistic treatment. It certainly would not confer end-regarding status on it.[8]

More important is a passage in which Kant seems to take the objective value of human beings to be what grounds the categorical imperative (at least in the humanity formula). In introducing the formula Kant indicates that if there is something whose existence has "absolute value," then "in it, and in it alone, would there be the ground of a possible categorical imperative," and he goes on to say that every rational being exists as such an end.[9] It may be that in principle, if we have or fully respect an end, we can consent to action toward us that accords with it; but the more important point, for Kant, seems to be that the actual value of persons (who may be developmentally or psychologically incapable of even conceiving an end) underlies the normative force of the categorical imperative, and there can certainly be a disparity between what respecting this value requires and what a person having such value actually could—as opposed to *should*—consent to. Whatever we say about how Kant is best

8. If one can take *pleasure* in being pained, this point might not apply; but it seems possible for another kind of masochist (if only by brain manipulation) to want pain wholly for its own sake when the person realizes no pleasure or other desirable result will accompany it. Such a desire is not plausibly considered rational.

9. *Groundwork*, sec. 428, 95 in Paton. For discussion of how this passage figures in realist versus constructivist interpretations of Kant's categorical imperative framework, see Kyla Ebels-Duggan, "Kantian Ethics," in Christian B. Miller, ed., *The Continuum Companion to Ethics* (London: Continuum, 2011).

read regarding the status of consent, my position on treatment of persons seems consistent with one plausible reading of his *Groundwork*.

II. Respect for Persons, Point of View, and Informed Rational Desire

A related point concerns respect, which can be clarified by my proposed account of treating a person as an end. Respecting you as a person implies an appropriate concern for your *point of view*, as determined by such factors as your deepest desires, your beliefs, your attitudes, and perhaps your welfare itself. Strictly speaking, the *agent* need not actually respect the person in question in the most common sense of 'respect': we may treat as ends people we think foolish and shallow. But the morally demanded respect for persons in question here does not require *esteem* or any attitude close to it.

The general idea here presupposes that our *view* on a matter need not well represent our interests or even our *point of view*. Our view may be unwarrantedly inferred from the latter or result from misleading advice.[10] Our point of view on a matter is often a complicated perspective determined by a multitude of beliefs, attitudes, and desires, and we are highly fallible about what holds or does not hold from that point of view. A point of view will sometimes have

10. That one's view, which is largely constituted by beliefs, need not represent one's point of view, which is much wider in constitution, can be seen from considerations that show the possibility of *rational* action against one's better judgment. In part, the idea is that the agent's *overall* normative grounds for action may not be reflected in the agent's judgment regarding it. Detailed argument and the relevant theory are given in my "Weakness of Will and Rational Action," *Australasian Journal of Philosophy* 68, 3 (1990).

internal tensions, such as a belief in compassion side by side with a conviction that punishment should be severe (a point of view might have some inconsistencies). For all that, normal adults are usually better able to speak for their points of view, at least regarding what they believe and what they want, than anyone else. Thus, even if I think you are making the wrong judgment from your point of view, to fail to give it due consideration as *your judgment* shows inadequate concern for your good and is prima facie wrong. The more reflective the judgment, the more consideration it merits (other things equal).

In a child or irrational adult, the relevant capacity for consent need not be realizable without growth or major psychological change. With permanently incompetent persons, proper concern with consent is hypothetical: roughly, appropriate to a rational person relevantly like them, where such likeness includes physical environment and social context, sources of pain and pleasure, and physical health. The requirement to treat someone as an end goes with the intuitive idea that such treatment characteristically expresses a kind of respect. The notion of respect, however, particularly taken morally, is not essential for characterizing end-regarding treatment. Indeed, my account of the latter can clarify the former at least as much as a good account of the former might clarify the latter. If there were not a basic kind of reason to treat persons as ends, their capacity to consent would not be morally as important as it is, and it would be less clear why they deserve a kind of respect.

Furthermore, if there were not a basic kind of reason to treat persons as ends, we would have far less to go on in determining just how heavily to weight actual consent to something that, because it is in a certain way misguided, would constitute failing to treat the persons in question as ends or even sink to treating them merely as means.[11] Taking consent, even certain kinds of hypothetical consent, as morally basic seems precluded by these points and appears to manifest a tendency to take what is at best an epistemic condition for *identifying* treatment as an end to be a ground of it. My points do not imply that consent, and especially a certain kind of hypothetical consent, is unimportant in determining what constitutes end-regarding treatment, but its importance is limited by the kinds of basic considerations that determine

11. Cf. Thomas E. Hill, Jr.: "the core idea of human dignity" is that "human beings are to be regarded as worthy of respect ... regardless of ... whether or not we disapprove of what they do." See "Basic Respect and Cultural Diversity," ch. 3 in *Respect, Pluralism, and Justice* (Oxford: Oxford University Press, 2000), 69. Moreover, "Endorsement under conditions of reasonable reflection, not mere sentiment, is what grounds values; and, significantly, the idea of *reasonable* reflection presupposes a willingness to listen to the voice, and heed the interests, of others" (68). It is not clear what substantive constraints this view would place on respect, reasonableness, interests, or treating persons as ends. Of such treatment he says, "the idea of humanity as an end in itself ... expresses the thought that human beings have dignity ... a special worth that conscientious agents must always take into account" (ch. 2, "A Kantian Perspective on Moral Rules," 42). In part, my project is to show that a non-technical notion of treating persons as ends is subject to constraints concerning the good of persons, where this is not just a procedural notion or a construct from their preferences. Hill's account of Kantian theory may leave room for many of my main points, but does not imply them. The kind of respectfulness account of the humanity formula Hill offers is discussed in detail (and Hill in particular considered) by Kerstein in *How to Treat Persons*, esp. ch. 2, and Kerstein also provides a detailed critical study of the consent approach to understanding merely instrumental and end-regarding treatment (see esp. chs. 3 and 4).

what *kind* of consent to actions toward ourselves is (or tends to be) *validating* of what is consented to in the first place.

The requirement to treat persons as ends is also clarified by noting one of its connections with informed rational desire. With special exceptions, we do not treat people as ends if we treat them in ways that we could not, if fully rational and adequately informed, want to be treated in the situation or could not want someone we care about to be treated in the relevant situation.[12] One exception would occur where we know some unusual preferences of the person which we do not share, say for being teased as a stimulus to witty repartee. Morality here recognizes rational self-interest—in which people may differ in part as a matter of sheer personal preferences—as one major guide to treating people in the ways it requires.[13]

12. One might be reminded here of Kant's calling "rational beings" those "who must themselves be able to share in the end of the very same action." See the *Groundwork*, sect. 68. Much depends on the criteria for being "able" to share; if he means *rationally* able—which is how we are to be able to universalize maxims under the categorical imperative—then his view of treating persons as ends could be consonant with my position. For a sketch of a different way to conceive the idea of persons' being ends in a non-consequentialist framework, see F. M. Kamm, "Non-Consequentialism, the Person as End-in-Itself, and the Significance of Status," *Philosophy & Public Affairs* 21, 4 (1992), esp. 358–359.

13. My view of treating persons as ends is probably compatible with the idea that such treatment entails respecting the *value* of their lives, on Scanlon's contractualist interpretation: "respecting the value of human (rational) life requires us to treat rational creatures only in ways that would be allowed by principles that they could not reasonably reject insofar as they, too, were seeking principles of mutual governance which other rational creatures could not reasonably reject." See *What We Owe to Each Other*, 106. One of my aims is to clarify some of the determinants of reasonableness

A plausible hypothesis here is that, other things equal, the more rational and integrated people are, the more their preferences should weigh in clarifying and constraining end-regarding treatment of them. A rational person can of course have some irrational desires; but the more integrated rational persons are—in terms of unity among beliefs, attitudes, desires, and other intentional elements—the less likely it is that they have any preferences that are not rational. Another factor is the importance of a preference for (or, better, in) the person. This is, roughly, the importance of satisfying it for realizing the person's good; it need not coincide with the importance of satisfaction in the person's judgment, which is not to imply that the person's judgment of importance need not be substantially weighed. The greater the importance of someone's preference in that person's good, the more pressure it exerts as a constraint on treating the person as an end. But even here, we must take account of the difference between someone's view of the importance of something and its actual importance in relation to the person's *overall* values—something it may be quite difficult for anyone, possibly including that individual, to judge.

Brief though our discussion of autonomy and preference has been, the basic idea that their value constrains what counts as end-regarding treatment of persons should now be clear.[14] The negative point here is that the good of persons is

and, negatively, to show that apart from some substantive standards, consent criteria are insufficient. In ch. 6 of *The Architecture of Reason* (Oxford: Oxford University Press, 2001), I offer an account of reasonableness and of some of those substantive standards.

14. Producing a detailed account would be difficult; treating persons as ends may differ from one person to another depending on their preferences and, to some extent, the agent's. But some modes of treatment are unacceptable regardless of preferences, just as some are acceptable regardless of preference. The difficult

not simply a construct out of their rational preferences, even if it can in some cases be described in terms of their *hypothetical* preferences understood so as to reflect such objective facts about human good as the badness of pain. But, positively speaking, we should acknowledge that an *element* in the good of persons is their freedom to realize certain of their desires. This point captures much of what is plausible in the idea that some kind of hypothetical consent is necessary for end-regarding treatment.

III. End-Regarding Treatment and Respecting Moral Rights

The notion of autonomy is often explicated partly in terms of the liberty rights of persons. I have stressed the way in which end-regarding treatment of persons respects their autonomy but have not explicated such treatment in terms of rights. Is end-regarding treatment of persons any different from treatment that respects their moral rights? If not, this indicates an important element in understanding the view that, as I have been arguing, end-regarding treatment entails caring about the good of the person in question. Suppose treating a person in a certain way is motivated by respect for the person's moral rights, in the sense that respect for some moral right of the person is at least a motivationally necessary condition for the action. Might we say, then, that rights-respecting treatment must be conduct in which someone is treated as an end and so cannot be merely instrumental conduct?[15]

question is how to specify the proper role of preferences, likes, stylistic inclinations, and other variable factors.

15. W. D. Ross suggests (without explicitly claiming) that (for Kant, at least) respecting rights is essential in end-regarding treatment. Rightly noting that Kant should not be read as prohibiting treatment of others as means, Ross adds, "What Kant insists on is

Rights-respecting treatment need not, in my view, be treatment of a person as an end, even if it typically cannot sink to being merely instrumental. One reason to think this is that respect for people's rights does not entail caring about their good for its own sake. Imagine a prison physician who abhors a (male) murderer but treats him well, relieving pain effectively, being considerate in manner, and so on. I grant that this would not normally be *merely* instrumental treatment, at least given the physician's having an adequate grasp of the person's rights and sufficient motivation to accord them. Such rights-guided motivation also implies major moral constraints on the relevant instrumental conduct. But is the patient treated as an end? That does not follow either from the treatment's not being merely instrumental or from its respecting rights. Is it true?

Much depends on how we conceive an apparently constitutive aim of medicine: relieving pain. If the physician aims at this as an end (and so "for its own sake"), that indicates non-instrumental motivation directed toward an aspect of the patient's good. In that case, the conduct *is* an instance of treating the patient at least partly as an end as I conceive such treatment. But suppose the physician does not care about his overall good, hence would not help with a kind of spiritual suffering that, though not a medical problem and not something he has no right to leave aside, is relievable by giving a kind of comfort verbally. Indifference to relieving such suffering, then, though within the physician's rights, would imply that the physician is not unqualifiedly treating the patient as an end. Even if the physician cares about achieving *a* good for the patient, say removing a ruptured appendix, for its own sake, this does not imply caring about *the* good of

that in treating others as means we must also have regard for their rights and interests." See *Kant's Ethical Theory* (Oxford: Clarendon, 1954), 49.

the patient for its own sake. Even apart from this, if the physician is doing the various good medical deeds only in order to respect the patient's rights—and so (for instance) is merely professionally satisfied by reducing the pain, as opposed to deriving satisfaction or positive feeling from this—then this is not treating the prisoner as an end. It is no doubt likely to be treating the prisoner *as if* he were an end, but that is a different matter.

The rights-respecting interpretation of treatment as an end is difficult to assess in part because it is not altogether clear just what rights we have. Theories of rights are highly variable. On many of them, however, we do not have a right to beneficent treatment that is not owed to us by promises or through special relationships such as we have with spouses and friends.[16] The physician has a promissory obligation to the prisoner (of a kind that grounds a far-reaching special right); but this is not a right to benevolence much less to any measure of altruism. To take a simpler case, I doubt that just anyone whose car is stalled and whom I can help has a right to have—as distinct from a right to request—my assistance. Surely I have a right—even if I ought not to exercise it—to take my disposition not to interact with that person as a sufficient reason not to, whereas this would not be true if I had promised to assist in such a case. Nor is my right simply stronger than the other person's; even if I do the wrong thing in not helping with the stalling problem, I do not violate the person's moral rights. Avoiding wrong-doing is a wider obligation than merely avoiding the violation of rights. Thus, if

16. A case to show that we do not have such rights is made in detail in my "Wrongs Within Rights," *Philosophical Issues* (*Noûs* supplementary volume) 15 (2005), 121–139. For a wider conception of rights see Nicholas P. Wolterstorff, *Understanding Liberal Democracy* (Oxford: Oxford University Press, 2012), e.g. 177–185.

it is always wrong to fail to treat someone I am interacting with as an end, that need not be because I would be violating a right. This applies even where I do have a special relationship with the person(s) in question. If, for instance, I am truly treating my students as ends, then I should do *more* for them than they have a right to have done.

Even on this restricted view of rights, however, on which what we ought to do for others goes beyond what they have a right to, it remains clear that rights-respecting conduct, even if not end-regarding, normally cannot be, or at least tends not to be, treating someone *merely* as a means. This point is important. But even if it is true that merely instrumental treatment is never fully rights-respecting, its contrast with rights-respecting treatment does not justify assimilating end-regarding treatment to rights-respecting treatment. Some cases of the former strongly suggest that the moral standard set by the demand to treat others as ends is higher than the demand to respect others' rights. In any event, this understanding, on which end-regarding treatment is not assimilated to rights-respecting treatment, makes both standards more useful than they would otherwise be. Indeed, for reasons that have already emerged, there are cases in which, as with overzealous parentalistic treatment of those we love, we fail to respect some of their rights even if we are treating them as ends.

IV. Conduct toward Persons versus Behavior Affecting Them

As common as the notion of treatment of persons is in the discourse of ethics, it is usually left unexplicated, especially from the point of view of moral psychology. The same holds for conduct toward others, of which treatment of them is the central case. Both notions can be better understood in the light of several further clarifications.

First (as illustrated earlier), not all action *affecting* others is a way of treating them or counts as conduct toward them. Affecting others is essentially causative in a way treatment of them need not be, and the former does not imply the latter. Recall the case of removing shoes in anticipation of a security request: this might affect others but, as normally done, is not a way of treating them or an instance of conduct toward them.[17] One might even deceive others without treating them in a particular way. Consider a realistic hairpiece: wearing this might affect others, even deceive them, without being a case of treating them in a certain way.

The example also shows something that is often missed: deception can be innocent, in a way lying cannot be. To be sure, if one promises one's spouse not to wear a hairpiece, then lying about having done so while away from home may be both reprehensible deception and bad treatment of the spouse. It would almost certainly also be a case of failing to treat as an end. Unsuccessful lying here—lying that does not deceive—would show the same thing; lying, unlike deception, is by its very nature wrong (though not indefeasibly so).

A further point is that the generic notion of treating persons in a certain way is not essentially causal (except insofar as any action is). More specifically, it need not cause any reaction, perception, or change in the person who is its object.

17. Similarly, entering the room might distract me; this need not be treating me a certain way, though it *affects* me. If I am conducting a class, it might be both treatment of me *and* morally significant. There are interesting borderline cases. Recall the case of surprising someone by singing on a dark street, thereby causing a heart attack. Is this treatment? What *kind* of singing we do, in volume, tone, and melody, matters. If certain kinds of singing are treatment of its hearer(s), the circumstances might determine whether they are prima facie wrong.

Consider a pathetic man who, with binoculars, spies on a woman he loves as she undresses for bed. This is a bad way to treat her (and certainly bad conduct toward her), even if he has no further aim than viewing her, he would never harm her, and the activity never affects her. Perhaps it is not entirely natural to call this a kind of treatment of her, but if she later discovered the activity, might she not properly say that spying on people is a bad way to treat them? It is certainly natural to call it treating her as an object of prurient interest. It smacks of objectification.

The case of the voyeur also illustrates another point, also shown by the case of detonating fireworks at dawn just for fun. Treatment of someone may be *neither* instrumental nor end-regarding. But the voyeur case, unlike the fireworks example, shows (as already suggested) something further: that treatment which is neither merely instrumental nor end-regarding need not be essentially causative toward its object: affecting the person in a negative or positive way. Instrumental treatment, however, does imply affecting another. One cannot treat someone as a means without in some way affecting the person, even if one fails to achieve the end. Treating as an end, by contrast, can be accomplished passively and at a distance. Think of benevolent vigilance. This might imply readiness to intervene in the causal order, but does not entail doing so. A parent could spy on an apparently suicidal child for the child's good, thereby treating the child as an end. This need not affect the child, since intervention may be unnecessary, and the treatment may be acceptable, if regrettable, parental conduct.[18]

18. Much should be said about just how action must be causative and about the general notion of treatment; my aims do not require going beyond the distinctions made to clarify merely instrumental vs. end-regarding treatment and their relation to moral appraisal. Note, too, that the idea that parental spying need

It should help to provide a tabular representation of part of my taxonomy. The following table does not represent every kind of morally significant conduct or action, but it does make clear that more kinds are countenanced if we distinguish merely from solely instrumental treatment in the way I propose:

Four Basic Kinds of Treatment of Persons			
Purely End-Regarding	*Mixed*	*Purely Instrumental*	*Not Instrumental or End-Regarding*
Wholly as an end	*Partly* as an end, *partly* as a means	*Solely* as a means *Merely* as a means	*Neither* as an end nor as a means

The second case is not often discussed in the literature of ethics, though many writers make ample room for the kind of mixed motivation it illustrates. The fourth case is rarely if ever acknowledged in discussions of merely instrumental and end-regarding treatment of persons. Our account shows that treatment of persons need have *no* instrumental element and that even when non-instrumental, it may be of the wrong kind to make it end-regarding. The voyeur spies on the woman he loves for its own sake and not instrumentally; but it is not done for her good. Similarly, as we saw earlier, speaking

not affect the child is consistent with the objectivity requirement on treating as an end: the activity can successfully aim at (and even contribute to) the child's *good* even without *affecting* the child in the ordinary causal sense implying a change in the child. Alternatively, one could say that affecting people's *status* (e.g. safety) without producing change in them *does* causally affect them. In any case, treating as an end is neither causative, nor a case of affecting a person, in the *way* treating merely as a means is.

in stentorian tones in a crowded restaurant is a bad way of treating others even if it is neither instrumental nor end-regarding. But since it constitutes *failing* to treat others as ends, it shows that, even if the moral assessment of treatment of others does not require its being either instrumental *or* end-regarding, that treatment may still be morally appraised in relation to at least one of those notions.

I reiterate that although merely instrumental treatment is like solely instrumental treatment in being motivated *only* instrumentally, the former is a special case of the latter and should be conceived partly in terms of additional morally significant, wrong-making elements. One might still argue that solely instrumental conduct is prima facie wrong in failing to be end-regarding; but that is a strong view. Consider asking an unknown neighbor in a dining hall to pass the salt. Suppose this is not motivated in the way required for end-regarding treatment. It may still be constrained by moral standards, and, so conceived, it does not appear prima facie wrong. Granted, it should be done politely, perhaps even respectfully. That is significant, but concerns its manner, whereas end-regarding treatment must have a certain kind of motivational basis, and that is not implied even by a respectful manner.

One might also reflect on whether leading a hermetical life is prima facie wrong in abandoning treating others as ends, at least where there is neither communication with other persons nor charitable contributions. Much depends on the kind of world in which such a life is chosen. I am inclined to hold that, unlike merely instrumental conduct, actions that simply do not represent treating people as ends may be morally neutral. Perhaps, however, the cases just mentioned are not treatment at all. In any event, there may be a conditional obligation such that, *if* conduct constitutes treatment of some person, then the agent has a prima facie obligation to treat the person at least partly as an end. I find this plausible, but leave it open.

————

Human conduct takes many forms. When it is social, it is usually constituted by the agent's treating someone in one or another way. Readers of Kant who, as he intended, take the categorical imperative framework as providing a fully comprehensive ethical standard, might think that all our conduct toward others is treatment of them or at least that all action for which we bear moral responsibility, whether retrospectively or prospectively, is treatment of someone. We have seen cases in which conduct is not treatment of a person at all, other cases in which social action does not imply treatment—even when it affects other people—and still other cases in which treatment does not (causally) affect its object. We have also seen how conduct can approach, without reaching, the highly negative status of unqualifiedly treating someone *merely* as a means. Neither the notion of end-regarding treatment nor the wider notion of morally desirable conduct is fully understandable in terms of consent by persons who are its object; but the value and autonomy of persons are important for understanding both notions, and an adequate account of the treatment of persons must take account of that fact.

Many points emerging so far also show how there is great variety in the ways in which we can treat people as ends. A constraint on our success in this is their conception of their own good, and the cases we have considered suggest that, other things being equal, the more rational that conception is, and the better integrated the person is, the stronger that constraint is. There are also objective, external constraints on treating persons as ends. Most obviously, such treatment requires caring about their pains and pleasures, but it also requires at least a disposition to care about their deepest concerns. These points belong to ethical theory, but they suggest a range of normative standards, some of which have been foreshadowed. They also indicate why end-regarding treatment tends to be rights-respecting, though the notion of rights-respecting treatment of persons is not equivalent to that of treating them as ends. In the final chapter, more will be said about the normative implications of the partial theory of conduct now in place.

8

CONDUCT, INTENTION, AND WILL

Conduct is three-dimensional. Its character is determined by the action(s) constituting its vehicle and behaviorally manifesting it, the reason(s) for the action(s), and the manner of performance of the action(s). Once we appreciate its three-fold constitution, we may wonder how conduct, as opposed to an action that is its vehicle, can be required of us in the way that is implicit in making it the target of imperatives, such as Kant's humanity formula. Positively, the formula tells us to treat persons as ends; its overt thrust is toward certain kinds of conduct, and (on at least one plausible reading) it implies that not to conduct ourselves accordingly is (prima facie) wrong. Negatively, it tells us to avoid merely instrumental treatment of persons, and we cannot adequately understand treating persons merely as means apart from the notion of conduct or some equivalent.

One way in which we may fulfill the negative injunction is not difficult to see. Abstaining from action prevents merely instrumental conduct. No vehicle, nothing carried. Moreover, other, unobjectionable actions may also suffice to accomplish the end for which one might be tempted to treat someone merely as a means. We can, then, avoid treating anyone merely as a means simply by abstaining from the relevant instrumental action and, sometimes, by finding alternative ways to achieve the same end. Abstaining may not be easy, but on the assumption that we can normally abstain

from an action if we will to do so, there is normally no puzzle
about one important way to fulfill the negative injunction
of the humanity formula: the path of abstention from (or
prevention of) instrumental action. It is not so easy, however,
to see how, on the one hand, we can treat others as means
in the way ordinary life often requires, yet, on the other
hand, avoid ever doing this *merely* instrumentally. The chal-
lenge is perhaps greatest where an agent who treats others
as means, as in employing them to do a job, strongly dislikes
them. Dislike tends to produces motivational patterns, and
sometimes callousness, that make at least *approaching* merely
instrumental treatment more likely than otherwise.

There is much that is puzzling about how we can fulfill
the positive injunction of the humanity formula. Can we
treat persons as ends on command, even self-command? It is
one thing to perform *actions* on command, or "at will"—thus
on inner command, one might think—but we surely cannot
in general evoke *motives* at will, much less bring it about at
will that, when we have them, we act on the basis of them or,
especially, on the basis of one we prefer to act on when we
have two or more motives that incline us toward the same
action. This makes it puzzling how, either on command or
simply by an effort of will, we can treat someone as an end.[1]

---

1. It may be clarifying to recall something brought out earlier
and especially relevant in preventing too strong an interpretation
of the injunction to treat persons as ends. Not all action *affecting*
persons implies treatment of them. The injunction thus leaves
open whether there are certain "minimal" ways of acting toward
others, as where one hands an usher a ticket, that do not constitute "treatment." In this light, Kant's end-respecting injunction is
perhaps best read as subject to more qualification than is usually
indicated in discussions of it: what it requires is that, *given* that
we do something constituting *treatment* of a person, the conduct in
question be treating the person as an end.

I. Motivational Self-Control
and the Scope of Intentions

A major question raised by these points about treatment of persons is this. If good conduct can require treating someone as an end, and this requires doing the right kind of thing for an appropriate reason and in a suitable way, how can we achieve such conduct? I may have direct control (within important limits) both of what I do and of how I do it; but, even if I have a motive I approve of and can do a deed appropriate to it, I may have a motive I disapprove of that favors the same action. Here I cannot at will *harness* an action to the favored motive—even focusing on the motive as I do the thing in question will not guarantee that I perform the action *on the basis of* the motive I approve of (as harnessing would achieve) rather than the other motive. Similarly, when I disapprove of a motive of mine that favors the same action, as where doing something positive for a friend disadvantages a competitor of mine, I cannot at will *unharness* it, i.e., detach it from the action so that I do not act even partly on that motive.

Setting Ourselves an End

Did Kant think otherwise? Granted he held that we can make something our end, but did he think we can act for a reason at will, and can we do so?[2] This is a difficult matter. Suppose

2. For some examples of Kant's view that we can make something our end, see, e.g., *The Doctrine of Virtue* and the *Groundwork*. In the latter he says, "Rational nature separates itself from all other things by the fact that it sets itself an end" (sec. 437, p. 105 in Paton). In *The Categorical Imperative*, W. D. Ross read Kant as thinking we can also perform acts, and sometimes have duties to perform acts, that harness actions to our ends—something I believe Kant did not think we can do at will. For discussion of this issue see my *Practical Reasoning and Ethical Decision*, e.g. 59–60.

that I can at will make something an end. By deciding to pursue something, I sometimes seem able to make it an end, at least where seeking it is consistent with the major elements in my motivational character. This presumably occurs when we successfully *resolve* to do something. Even if I do resolve to pursue an end I thereby come to want for its own sake, it does not follow that, if I do something that I believe will or may realize the end, I do it *for* that reason: in order to realize the end I resolved to pursue. As Kant saw, we might have two reasons to do something, one of duty and one of inclination, and be unable to tell which, if either, is the basis *on* which we act.[3]

Granted, one can intelligibly say things like 'I know it will be difficult, but I intend to help him because I promised to' (where this means roughly: because of my promising to help him, I intend to do so). But 'I intend to help him because I promised to' would normally be a statement of intention to do something together with an explanation of why one has the intention (or it might be an indication of the basis on which one would like to do it). It is not equivalent to 'I have an intention with the content: to-help-him-because-I-promised-to'; nor is it clear that there is any content appropriate to constitute the object of such an intention.

The question of the extent and dimensions of our motivational self-control is multifaceted. We must consider several

---

3. In the *Groundwork* Kant makes clear that we sometimes cannot tell for which of two aligned reasons we act. He says, e.g., that even if without the moral motive of duty we find nothing that "could have been strong enough to move us to this or that good action ... we cannot infer from this with certainty that it is not some secret impulse of self-love which has actually ... been the cause genuinely determining our will." See the *Groundwork*, sec. 407 (p. 74 in Paton); cf. the more nuanced comment on the matter in sec. 397 (p. 65 in Paton).

questions. First, what is it to set an end, in the sense in which, when we have done so, citing the end can explain an action of ours and our setting the end bears on our moral responsibility for conduct toward others, say by making it deliberate? Second, what capacities might we have to see to it that our actions are grounded in the ends appropriate to them? And third, how might we ensure that our actions are performed in a manner that befits the overall context, including our end(s) in acting, our action(s) toward someone, and facts about the person(s)? These questions cannot be answered fully without information from empirical psychology, but philosophical reflection can provide a framework for accommodating various kinds of results that may emerge from psychological studies. I begin with conceptual points concerning the setting of ends.

Setting an end is one thing, pursuing it is another, and pursuing it for the right kind of reason is still another. I can resolve to support a friend in a custody matter. Resolutions and vows are ways of setting ends. Promising is another way: what we sincerely promise to do normally becomes an end we undertake to realize. Weakness of will can of course prevent my achieving an end I have set. Moreover, if I do achieve it, that may not be by a path I approve of, say, in order to help the friend's child. For I may also have another reason: to create indebtedness in my friend. Having two or more reasons for an action—or for a kind of conduct toward others—is not like having two or more incompatible paths to different destinations, where one cannot take both. It is better compared with having two or more engines linked in tandem, each with sufficient power to propel our railroad car on the same track. Suppose that just as we can often act at will, we can activate forward movement by a throwing a master switch. If we do this, we might hope that the economy of the design calls for just one engine to propel our car; but—especially where they run quietly and are wired to run together unless disconnected from one another—we cannot assume that the preferred engine yields our movement, or tell whether both together do. Even an engine that pollutes may do it imperceptibly.

We should also notice that the idea of setting an end encompasses a number of different possibilities. The end can be behavioral, thus an object of intention, decision, or resolution, to act. But an end can also be as broad as formation of a disposition or even a trait. One could resolve to be loving or, related to this broad resolution, one might resolve to adopt a practice, say of regularly treating one's employees, or people in general, better. Here success would result in producing—more likely by a combination of actions rather than by a single act of will—a sufficiently strong disposition to engage in the kind of conduct in question. One could vow to cast off pretense and become forthright—a matter that requires eliminating an old pattern and acquiring a new one. Here full success would result in uprooting one trait and implanting another.

These self-reformational results are all realizable *by* what we do; but none is simply action that any normal person can perform at will. Consider the aim of treating people better, understood as, in good part, treating them as ends. To bring this pattern of treatment about, one must not only come to do certain things but must characteristically do them for the right kind of reason. This pattern can be brought about, but it is not itself action (and, as suggested above, I do not see that Kant must be read as taking it to be action), as opposed to setting, as an end, the practicing of this kind of conduct. Let me explain.

On my view (as indicated earlier), '*A*-ing for *R*' does not designate an act-type. If we can bring about instances of acting for a particular reason, it is not directly, but by doing things that yield this complex causal sequence. Perhaps the simplest example of indirectly bringing about this sequence would be appropriate brain manipulation, at least on the assumption that neural states of some kind are causally sufficient for production both of desires and of actions performed on the basis of those desires. Normally, by an exercise of self-monitoring combined with moral self-discipline, we can strengthen both our motivation to achieve certain ends and our sensitivity to why and how we do what we aim at doing. But there are many questions here, both conceptual and empirical. Among the conceptual questions is whether strengthening our motivation is an action proper or (as seems more likely) something else that is realizable by action. Among the empirical questions is how best to strengthen certain motives in a given kind of life. My main concern is not to answer these questions but simply to sketch the range of possibilities for self-improvement open to us and, in relation to some of those possibilities, the scope of our moral responsibility for conduct.

The Manner of Interpersonal Conduct

So far, my focus in this chapter has been chiefly on the motivation and act-types constituent in conduct. But as many of our examples have shown, the manner in which we act can be morally significant. This is particularly so in interpersonal conduct, though manner is not without significance in some solitary conduct. Suppose you are a manager who must lay off an employee. Even if you do not regret having to do it, you can do it sympathetically, in terms of voicing, gesture, and wording, or instead dryly, expressionlessly—even triumphally if you have been waiting for an opportunity. There is a huge range of ways to do the deed. The range becomes richer as the act in prospect becomes more complex or more extended in time. But there are limits. Without actually regretting that I must do the deed, I probably cannot do it regretfully—at least not without hypocrisy. If I want to do it regretfully *and* sincerely, I may, as I approach doing it, think of regrettable aspects of it in hopes of producing regret that will be evident in my manner of action. But this is not, in my experience, a good way to evoke a corresponding emotion or desire. The case apparently confirms that producing motivation and other attitudinal elements at will is generally not possible for normal agents.

Our behavioral *skills* also limit our capacities for achieving certain manners of action: some people can do almost nothing elegantly, others almost nothing casually, still others almost nothing cruelly.[4] Nonetheless, for a huge range of manners of action, we commonly have direct control of whether or not we act in the relevant way, and, by self-discipline and practice, we can apparently broaden this range considerably. We can thus be in a better position to treat others as ends.

It is clear, then, that our control of our future conduct is apparently sufficient to sustain wide moral responsibility for it. This applies, in ways I have illustrated, to treatment of persons as ends. One important thing that the limitations on our voluntary control of our treatment of others shows is that—as stressed throughout this book—the requirements of ethics are not just "actional." For in our treatment of persons, as in other kinds of behavior, our moral responsibility

---

4. As the use of adverbs here suggests, perhaps all manners of action can be adverbially described. But even if all actions admit of adverbial modification (whether or not the agent can in fact realize the manner in question), not all adverbial modifications concern elements that are in the scope of an agent's control. Some concern the environment, as where dry twigs on our path result in our walking noisily; others concern psychological factors we cannot directly control, as the absence of regret in the layoff example shows. Still other constraints on the manner of action are situational and may easily vary: I cannot (orally) communicate a layoff privately if I have no private space in which to do it.

extends to things we can affect that are not actions at all, much less actions we can perform at will. This is not to say that we can fulfill moral requirements *without* action, which I take to imply performing some basic action. But ethics requires (of at least the vast majority of us) certain kinds of treatment of persons, and treatment of persons is conduct and not just action.

Must we say, then, that contrary to what seems almost obvious, we can be morally required to do what we cannot intend to do? I do not believe we must draw this paradoxical conclusion. We should say instead that although what we can intend must be *achievable* by the performance of one or more actions, by conduct, or by producing a state of affairs (such as the good state of being up to date with one's professional responsibilities), it need not itself be ordinary action—or, at least, there is a correct way of specifying the content of an intention that does not constitute an ordinary act-reporting phrase. These points can be brought out clearly by exploring something familiar and often too easily assumed to be well understood—the commandment to love one's neighbor as oneself.

II. Moral Requirements and the Content of Intention

The injunction to treat persons as ends is significantly analogous to the famous commandment to love one's neighbor as oneself (Matthew 22:37–39; cf. Mark 12:29–31; Leviticus 19:18; and Deuteronomy 6:4). In a normal rational person who lives in a community, achieving the latter surely entails realizing the former: realizing end-regarding treatment of one's "neighbor." The former, moreover, though it does not entail loving a person treated as an end, may well be best exemplified by treatment that expresses what has been called agapistic love; and that, in turn, entails (non-instrumentally) caring about the good of those one loves.[5] This is not to say just what constitutes appropriate self-love. Here I simply assume that an essential element in it is end-regarding: caring about one's own good for its own sake.

A related directive—on the plausible assumption that commanding and promising have the same kinds of objects—is contained in the common marriage ceremony in which one promises, and presumably can and should intend, to love. But love is not an action. So, if we take the commandment to love to be one we can fulfill by our actions, we must apparently conclude that either love can be intended despite not being an action or that to *say* one intends to love is a way of saying (roughly) that one intends to do the things appropriate to expressing and nurturing love. I find both interpretations in need of explication. In any case, if one can literally intend to love, not just any intention with this content would be directly action-guiding in the way appropriate to intention. One certainly cannot rationally intend to love without having at least intentions, or sufficiently strong desires, with contents that include some appropriate subset of the deeds in the categories of expressing and nurturing love.

Three Interpretations of the Intention to Love Someone

It will help in understanding the injunction to treat persons as ends if we further explore the motivational elements required for its fulfillment. Imagine a physician who, annoyed

---

5. Kant clearly saw similarity between the commandment to love our neighbors as ourselves and his requirement that we treat others as ends. See, e.g., *The Critique of Practical Reason*, trans. Lewis White Beck (Indianapolis, IN: Bobbs-Merrill, 1958), 85–88 (secs. 82–85).

with a hypochondriacal patient, resolves to treat the patient during an office visit as an end rather than simply as a professional burden, where the vehicle of the conduct is doing a careful examination. We might say that the resolution to treat the patient as an end is, like a command, *executed* or perhaps *obeyed* by the (intentional) performance of the required act-types, but *fulfilled* only if the performance is motivated by caring about the patient's good for its own sake. One might say that when the resolution is merely executed, the letter but not the spirit of the resolution is carried out, but that is not quite right: here the spirit—as manifested in motives and manners—is part of the letter. Again, the difficulty is to understand what counts as the content of the intention to treat as an end, or (as seems to entail this) the content of the intention to love someone else as oneself, where motivation *is* part of the letter.

Recall the two understandings of the neighborly love commandment. We might clarify the first understanding, on which we can intend to love—or at least can have an intention whose content is roughly expressed by 'to love'—along these lines. We might widen the kind of behavioral content the object of intention can have and take it to include at least mainly bringing about states of affairs of any sort within a broad affectional range, such as having an abiding love for someone. Call this the *affectional-pattern interpretation*: the content of what we call the intention to love is roughly the higher-order aim to bring about or to sustain (or both) the kind of pattern that manifests loving one's neighbor. (We should include here intention to *sustain* the pattern; this accommodates those who think they already instantiate the pattern and so would not intend to bring it about anew.) Since bringing about is action (though often not basic action if it ever is), this interpretation accommodates the idea that the objects of intention are acts of some kind, and it also allows us to deny that 'intend to love' expresses an intention whose precise object is an emotion, though without more explication we leave open what non-acts, if any, the intention to love encompasses.

On the second interpretation—call it the *conjunctive interpretation*—we also retain the plausible idea that the objects of intention are acts and activities, but take 'to love' in the injunction to designate (elliptically) an open-ended conjunction of actions and activities of a loving kind, presumably including, if in some implicit way, a broad notion like bringing about.[6] The difference is that on the affectional pattern interpretation a behavioral umbrella notion like *bringing about* expresses the content of the intention, whereas, on the conjunctive interpretation, 'to love' is conceived more concretely as a shorthand for a perhaps indefinite list of specific kinds of deeds, and no such umbrella notion need figure centrally, though it may. In practice, roughly the same conduct might be expected from people who internalize the commandment on either interpretation. Moreover, for different people, or for the same person at different times, one or the other interpretation of the agent's intentional state may be preferable.

Our purposes here do not require a choice between these two understandings of intention of love, though the second, conjunctive one, is more in line with how many married people would explain what they intend if asked how

---

6. A conjunction of intentions might also fit the psychology of the agent, sometimes better, and it may be that in different situations one or the other case better fits that psychology. Certainly, if what is, say, resolved, is a course of action that is constituted by doing dozens of discrete things the agent in some sense foresees, it may be more plausible to take the agent to intend to A, and to B, and to C, etc., as opposed to having a single intention to A and B and C, etc. With certain possible exceptions, we would expect the same behavior to go with either of the corresponding ascriptions.

they conceive the content of the marital promise to love. They intend to live in harmony with the other, to share resources, to assist during illness, and so forth. The more we have thought about the relevant matter, the richer the conjunctive intention is likely to be. Even if we can intend only acts and activities, either understanding of the content of promising—and correspondingly of the injunction to treat persons as ends—makes it possible to see how we can intend what we must if we are properly said to intend to treat persons as ends. Moreover, either is available to Kantian ethics in relation to the humanity formula. Both interpretations apply to the intention to treat others as ends, much as they apply to the commandment to love one's neighbors. As to the universalizability formulas (whether in Kantian or other ethical theories), the options presented here regarding the content of intention can be used to clarify specification of what is to be universalized, for instance an act-type, or conjunction of act-types, described in relation to a context, as where one resolves: to keep my promises unless doing so would in the circumstances be bad for the promisee.

Another reason we need not choose between these two interpretations is that there is a third, which encompasses both and seems superior to either taken by itself. Although intentions are most commonly *to do,* there are also intentions *that,* say that one's children become well educated. These may have indefinite content, at least regarding the acts one does or would take to realize the object intended. Such *subjunctive intentions* (as we might call them) always imply some intentions to do, but they do not require as detailed agential conception of the acts in their scope, if indeed they require any specific act-type in that role. We could take commandments to love someone and to treat persons as ends as requiring *that* one be loving toward the person in question and *that* one achieve treating persons as ends, where these construals are understood in the open-ended way I have indicated, concerning act-type, motivation, and manner of action. Intentions *that* have indefinitely wide content, including the kind indicates by infinitives, such as intending to be respectful of others; and the intention that one treat others as ends may imply intentions with the behavioral content indicated on either of the first two readings. Given these options, we can retain the idea that one cannot be commanded to do what one cannot intend, but we must clarify this by indicating the kind of intention and the elements and range of its content.

None of these options for understanding an ethics that is like Kant's in emphasizing conduct as well as acting on principles implies that acting-for-a-particular-reason is itself an act-type or that *only* treatment-types (such as treating someone as an end) are genuinely objects of moral obligation. The assumption that, for Kant, they are the only genuine objects of obligation—perhaps a natural assumption given his taking his various formulations of the categorical imperative to be equivalent—may be one reason why he is sometimes taken to be committed to conceiving acting for a particular reason and acting on a specific maxim, to be types of action. But must this equivalence be preserved to do justice to Kant's overall view? Might one take the universalizability formulations to be directed toward determining what act-types are obligatory and the humanity formula as indicating obligatory and wrongful treatment-types?[7] This is a possibility I cannot pursue here; it is enough to indicate how, by pursuing it, a broadly Kantian ethic might be shown to have the additional power of complementary formulas rather than just the lesser benefit of terminological variants of a single one.

---

7. Something close to this is suggested, or in any case made readily understandable, by Stratton-Lake, op. cit., e.g. 45–51.

It may be that some people, by virtue of their particular psychological constitution, can form intentions to do what is required to treat a person as an end only where they conceive the commitment as directed toward bringing about a certain range of deeds in a certain way. They might think of their commitment as bringing about a pattern of conduct. Others may have a more concrete understanding of their commitment and conceive it conjunctively, in terms of an open-ended list of kinds of acts that they can readily perform and that they take to be normally motivated in some appropriate way. Suppose that, in either instance or both—i.e., on the pattern or the conjunctive interpretation of the injunction to treat persons as ends—a case can be made that the content of commands and promises need not, even when properly spelled out, be acts. This certainly holds where intentions *that* are the crucial elements whose content indicates commitment to the commands or promises. Nonetheless, fulfilling commands and promises—at least fulfilling their letter—is done *by* our actions under certain motivational and behavioral conditions.

Fulfillment of Conduct Requirements

On the assumption I favor, that what we are commanded to do is, even if only implicitly, constituted by acts (including higher-order acts and activities), we can still give a reasonably clear interpretation of the imperative to obey humanity formula, the love commandments, promises to love, and the like. But on any plausible interpretation of the injunction to treat persons as ends, we must suppose that complete fulfillment, as opposed to overt behavioral conformity, is not achieved just by actions of an appropriate act-type, or even those actions performed in appropriate ways. Complete fulfillment is achieved only by the relevant deeds being based on end-regarding motivation—and being done in an appropriate way; in short, by what I am calling *conduct*. Bringing about good conduct requires a measure of self-understanding and self-control. Achieving it may be difficult, and the difficulty varies with different people and, for anyone, with different kinds of situation. Reducing that difficulty is one aim of moral education, though there is no formula for doing so and, in my judgment, no adequate substitute for good role-modeling.

It should also be stressed that even though conduct is not exhausted by action, most of our interpersonal actions manifest conduct, and action is its perceptible element. Given that conduct has action as its vehicle and as its most commonly manifest facet, it is no surprise that conduct can be commanded and required. If we can readily perform the relevant action, and especially if we have considerable control of the manner of our performing it, we can at least *begin* to fulfill the requirement the command imposes. Moreover, we apparently can sometimes extinguish hatred at will or, at will, do for someone a deed that we are reasonably sure we will in fact do for an end-regarding reason when the occasion for action comes.

It is significant that control of the manner in which one performs an action may also be something one can achieve either at will or by doing something readily brought about at will. If I cannot always, at will, be gentle toward someone I am criticizing, I can at will soften my voice and select unthreatening words. Moreover, for morally upright agents, doing the right thing in the right way surely often flows from and is based on the right reason(s). The likelihood that it is so based may indeed be increased by forming and retaining an intention, especially a reflective intention, to do it in a manner that is consonant with its type. Even if end-regarding conduct in which one does the right kind of thing in an acceptable manner is insufficiently frequent in everyday life, such conduct—which often prominently exemplifies acting morally—is typical of a good many people and usually possible for normal persons in much of their lives.

III. Conduct Requirements and the Love Commandments

Love is broadly attitudinal and emotional, rather than a kind of conduct. But acting lovingly is akin to acting morally and at least typically *is* a kind of conduct. Since the directive to love one's neighbors is plausibly taken to call for loving conduct, which is end-regarding, it is fruitful to consider this directive in ways we have not yet explored, especially by comparing the commandment to love our neighbors with the positive directive of the humanity formula, which requires end-regarding conduct. Recall the problem. It is natural to be puzzled by the commandment to love because, on the one hand, love is not an action but, on the other, it is (as we have seen) not clear exactly what is meant by commands whose objects appear not to be actions. I can raise my hands at will, and it makes sense to command me to raise them, as well as to do deeds that are accomplished *by* my raising them. But consider being commanded to love a person one hates—or even to treat the person as an end. Does a command to love even make clear sense as applied to someone we do not love? I have suggested that, properly understood, it does and have illustrated how. Let me indicate some ways to fulfill the command that apply on any of the understandings we have explored regarding the intention to obey it: the pattern and conjunctive interpretations or the view that the relevant intention is broader still—to the effect *that one love,* where this phrase encompasses both acts and states of affairs they may be aimed at realizing.

   An important point here is that even if we do not have direct positive control over our emotions, and hence cannot bring them into being at will, there *are* cases in which we have direct negative control over them. I cannot fear at will, but I sometimes can overcome fear by an act of will—by resolving not to be afraid, to put it in a more natural way. This bears some similarity to holding my breath for a medical examination. Something similar might apply to extinguishing hatred at will.

Even apart from the possibility of doing at will things that, like eliminating hatred, make way for love to grow, there are of course *acts* of love. Here we find no exact parallel in treating persons as ends. Granting that acts of love, at least viewed simply as intentional action, tend to be vehicles of end-regarding treatment (though they can be hypocritically mimicked), the range of eligible act-types to serve as vehicles is both wide and also indeterminate at least at the edges. But just as, *without* action, at least in the heart and mind, love is in a sense *unrealized*, we cannot treat others as ends if we do nothing at all in relation to them.

Acts of love, then, like treating persons as ends, may be commanded and, in some cases, performed at will. But the acts that well deserve the name, those that merit being called acts of love by the conduct they partly constitute rather than by their appearance, may not always be achievable at will, if they ever are. Similarly, the conduct that rises to treating someone as an end, though it may be morally required, occurs only when, through virtue or circumstance or some combination of favorable elements, the right kind of action and the right kind of motive are connected in the right way, and the action is performed in a manner appropriate to its type, its motivation, and its context.

With conduct, whether it is loving or simply a case of treating someone as an end, its *constitution* includes motivational grounding of the action that is its vehicle; its appearance is a matter of the act-type salient in it. For instance, making a sacrifice, in the strict sense, for a child or a friend must, if it is an act of love, be achieved by action for an other-regarding reason, and it requires forgoing something one wants. Making a sacrifice is not a matter of mere behavior, such as writing a check. More generally, the deeds that, typically, represent love may certainly be commanded; but if they are done simply *on command*, they are no longer truly acts of love and may not represent treating anyone as an end. They are at best *loving kinds of acts*, but they do not bespeak love.[8]

Consider again promises to respect and to honor. These are also appropriate to the wide human commitment that goes with an ethics of conduct, of which I take an ethics of love to be, in most forms, an instance. Like acts of love, respecting and honoring others are also not a matter of mere behavior. Promising to honor someone is surely one way of setting an end. A sincere promise is accompanied by formation of an intention whose object is either the act promised or, in some way, bringing about the conduct promised, as may apply to the promise to love. A resolution to do something, such as a supportive deed for a friend, is another way to set an end. But such volitional undertakings do not guarantee success. They need not produce action at all. When they do, they may yield actions that only give the impression of being vehicles of the intended conduct, say treating someone as end through one's acts of love. Mixed motivation is also possible, as when someone is treated partly as an end but also partly as a means to fulfilling a selfish purpose. Partial success is of course preferable to utter failure, but the full demands of ethics—in Kant, in virtue ethics, in the most

8. Much of what is said in this section bears on what is required by an ethics of love. For an account of the ethics of love see Frances Howard-Snyder, "On These Hang All the Law and the Prophets," *Faith and Philosophy* 22, 1 (2005).

plausible intuitionist theories, and arguably in a comprehensive utilitarian view[9]—require the kind of success constituted by treating persons as ends.

———

The ethics of conduct focuses on its three dimensions: action, motivation, and manner. Right action alone does not entail morally good conduct. Even morally good conduct need not manifest good character. But if good moral conduct is prevalent in someone's interpersonal behavior, it is at least likely that good moral character underlies it. The scope of moral appraisal extends to all of the variables we have considered. Even on the view that we are morally responsible, directly, just for our actions, these foreseeably affect our conduct, attitudes, emotions, motivation, and character. We can be held responsible, then, for treating others as ends, even if this is not in general something we can achieve at will. Loving our neighbors is certainly not something achievable at will, but there is much we can do to make it possible for us. Avoiding treating others merely as means, or even approaching that reprehensible way of relating to them, is far less difficult, and for some people it is quite natural. But good conduct, especially as realized by treating persons as ends, and certainly good character, require much more. The everyday examples we have explored, however, show that end-regarding treatment and good character are not just ideals but moral requirements that normal persons can at least often meet.

9. For John Stuart Mill's view of how motives are ethically important, see *Utilitarianism* fn. 2 (which appeared in the 2nd ed.). Cf. Sidgwick, op. cit., 208. Robert M. Adams and Julia Driver have also written on this matter. See his *A Theory of Virtue: Excellence in Being for the Good* (Oxford: Clarendon Press, 2006) and her *Uneasy Virtue* (Cambridge: Cambridge University Press, 2001).

CONCLUSION

Ethics is concerned with what we ought to do and, especially in the virtue-ethics tradition, with how we ought to *be*—with what kinds of persons we should be. But its scope is even wider. We can be ethically well constituted and do the right things, but not always do them for the right reasons—a failure in the dimension of the moral worth of actions and one that can befall even virtuous agents. An ethically well-constituted person may also on various occasions do the right things in the wrong way—a failure in the adverbial dimension of normative appraisal, that of the manner of action. A full-scale ethical theory should incorporate an ethics of conduct; it can then encompass all three of these dimensions of behavior—act-type, motivation, and manner of performance—as it should, given that the scope of moral responsibility includes conduct as constituted by elements in each dimension. The moral appraisal of persons and their behavior is incomplete without assessment in at least these three domains.

If the scope of our will—roughly, the range of things we can intend and rationally hope to bring about through what we do at will—were narrower than it is, an ethics of conduct might be too demanding. But it should now be clear that directly or indirectly, we can do much to bring it about that we regularly treat others as ends and steadfastly avoid treating anyone merely as a means. Moral education can be viewed as in good part an attempt to create a reliable tendency to conduct oneself so. It may be guided by the relevant standards of conduct, of course, without their being conceptualized in the kinds of terms in which I have discussed them here. To think that moral education and ordinary moral appraisal require such sophistication would be intellectualist in a way this book is not. It would be to project into ordinary conscientious thinking the use of a number of concepts needed for a philosophical understanding of ethics but not required for moral agency. People can achieve considerable subtlety in their thinking and their moral conduct without exercising those concepts and, often, quite without self-consciousness.

As I have represented the scope of moral responsibility, it is as wide as our volitional capacities permit. If this seems too strong a view, recall that we can treat others as ends even if we also treat them (partly) as means. Human life requires much conduct that characteristically has multiple purposes. As to avoiding treatment of someone merely as a means, this can be accomplished by abstention from the action(s) that would manifest such treatment. Our negative volitional power is wide, and clearly wider than our positive volitional power. Certainly we can at will (normally) abstain from what we see would be, or would approach, merely instrumental treatment, though in general we cannot at will bring it about that our treatment of someone—especially where we believe it benefits us—is end-regarding. If, as one might think in comparing negative and positive obligations, the negative side of morality is ethically more important than the positive side, then we may take it that nature, in determining our volitional endowment, has cooperated with the needs of morality—or, perhaps, morality has cooperated with nature.[1]

1. This issue is connected with the contrast in moral stringency between negative and positive duties, something addressed by Kant, Ross, and many others. A detailed case that, other things

There is one more thing to say to conclude my account of the two important notions, negative and positive, of treating persons merely as means and treating them as ends—the two that are among the most important general notions in an ethics of conduct, as distinct from an ethics of rules and from virtue ethics. On the proposed account of treating persons merely as means, that notion grounds prima facie prohibitions. However infrequent such treatment may be in morally decent persons, we can see why it constitutes a negative ethical standard: conduct realizing it is prima facie wrong, often blatantly wrong. It is commonly exploitive, and, at least in spirit, it is callous even if it benefits the person so treated. By contrast, the notion of treating persons as ends constitutes a positive ethical standard; and, as is clear from our account of it, it is a basis for positive judgments of conduct even if (as I have left open) it is not prima facie obligatory in all interpersonal conduct. The total absence of such treatment would immensely attenuate the influence of morality in human life.

If merely instrumental treatment and end-regarding treatment are explicated as I propose, they can better serve as guides in ethics. They can be among the anchors of moral judgment. Both are understandable independently of Kant's conception of them and even of moral concepts or prior moral judgments. Partly for that reason, this book provides independent support for at least some of the overall uses to

equal, certain of the former, such as the duty not to kill, are more stringent than "corresponding" positive duties, such as the duty to save (and so not to let die), is given in my paper "The Moral Rights of the Terminally Ill," in John W. Davis, Barry Hoffmaster, and Sarah Shorten, eds., *Contemporary Issues in Biomedical Ethics* (Clifton, NJ: The Humana Press, 1979), 43–62. Later work by Kurt Baier, *The Rational and the Moral Order* (Peru, IL: Open Court, 1995) and Judith Thomson, "Turning the Trolley," *Philosophy and Public Affairs* 36, 4 (2008), 359–374, supports the view I defended there.

which Kant and others have put these notions in grounding moral judgments.[2] We understand what it is to use an
instrument solely as a means and also what it is to use one
merely as such, where its fate is of no concern to us and we
are disposed not to become non-instrumentally concerned
with it. This understanding and the descriptive judgments
we make on the basis of it do not epistemically depend on
moral judgment. Knowledge of conduct as merely instrumental grounds moral judgments; it does not have a prior,
evidential dependence on them. We also have a good understanding, and considerable knowledge, of many descriptive,
non-moral sufficient conditions for contributing to a person's good, such as reducing suffering and enhancing rational capacities. Knowledge of conduct as end-regarding, like
knowledge of it as merely instrumental or approaching that,
can also anchor moral judgments.

There are, then, many uses of descriptive factual criteria to clarify moral judgments grounded in ascriptions of
merely instrumental or of end-regarding treatment. These
criteria clarify the injunctions to avoid the former and
achieve the latter, and they provide an objective basis for a
wide range of moral judgments. Endorsing the injunctions
does not require taking them to account for appraising *all*

2. For indications of how to interpret Kant here, see the works
cited herein by Hill, Korsgaard, O'Neill, and Timmermann, and
also Karl Ameriks, "Kant on Good Will," ch. 7 in his *Interpreting
Kant's Critiques* (Oxford: Oxford University Press, 2003); Paul
Guyer, "Ends of Reason and Ends of Nature: The Place of
Teleology in Kant's Ethics," *Journal of Value Inquiry* 36 (2002),
161–168; Stratton-Lake, op. cit., esp. chs. 2–4; and Houston Smit
and Mark Timmons, "Kant's Grounding Project in *The Doctrine
of Virtue*," in M. Timmons and S. Baiasu, eds., *Kant on Practical
Justification: Interpretive Essays* (Oxford: Oxford University Press,
2013), 229–268.

obligations. But these injunctions do provide comprehensive and intuitively compelling standards that clarify obligations in practice and unify more specific ethical principles—in education, politics, business, and other domains.

Moreover, because the injunctions provide standards of *conduct* and not specifications of ordinary act-types to be realized or avoided, they reflect the depth and scope of morality in a way mere behavioral standards do not, say the prohibition of killing on the negative side and, on the positive side, the requirement to keep promises. Morality reaches below the surface of action. It appraises the motivation and manner of what we do. It calls for both self-assessment and appraisal of others. It holds for institutions as well as individuals, at least insofar as institutional obligations are a matter of the obligations of individuals with crucial institutional roles. It guides the formation and reformation of character, supports other-regarding motivation, and constrains the manner of our treatment of others and not just the act-types represented by our deeds toward them.

The conception of the treatment of persons developed here provides resources not only for clarifying and, in significant ways, supporting Kantian ethics, but also for clarifying and supporting intuitionist pluralism of the kind articulated by Ross. Intuitionists in ethics, like many other moral theorists, posit obligations of, for instance, beneficence that they do not consider properly fulfilled—fulfilled in the way that represents good character—if the actions are not motivated in a way that represents good conduct. These resources are also pertinent to appraising elements in virtue ethics, and they are important for the assessment of consequentialism. Consequentialists, if they seek to do full justice to intuitively plausible moral judgments, should take account of the notions of treating someone merely as a means and of treating persons as ends; Kantian ethics should be informed by taking into account a different understanding of these notions than so far provided by its proponents; and intuitionist pluralism is far more plausible if it can employ these notions in unifying and clarifying its disparate moral demands.

It should be clear, then, that the partial theory of conduct developed in this book has broad implications for ethical theory. As I have already indicated in various ways, on the theory I am developing, ethics should be broadly conceived as concerned with far more than acts and their consequences, and in that point my view contrasts with at least many utilitarian approaches. Ethics should indeed be concerned with far more than even those consequences together with the intrinsic moral significance of motivation, something important in Kantian ethics, and also with much more than virtue and its behavioral manifestations, as for much of virtue ethics. The theory of conduct concerns all of these elements together with *manners* of action—with what I have called the adverbial dimension of ethics.

The conduct theory I have proposed, centering on treatment of persons as the primary case, also has implications for normative ethics. Most generally, I have shown how important it is to give weight to the notion of conduct in moral appraisal of persons and their deeds. Comprehensive moral appraisal of behavior should be three-dimensional, encompassing the three elements constitutive of conduct: act-types, motivation, and elements in the adverbial dimension of action. That such three-dimensional appraisal is of great importance may not be controversial in ethics. But there will be disagreement about whether normative objectivity is, in the ways I have described, crucial for understanding end-regarding treatment and about the limitations I have argued objectivity places on the moral role of consent. Those matters are among the many we have explored that demand further reflection.

As important as conduct is for ethics, I do not consider it the only concern of an adequate normative ethics. We cannot articulate the requirements of morality without specifying act-types as right or wrong and states of affairs, including the consequences of actions, as good or bad. I have not meant to downplay the importance of either the theory of obligation as applied primarily to action or, certainly, the theory of value as applied primarily to experiences and states of affairs. But we cannot morally appraise people or adequately guide human action without considering both their motivational character and how they do what they do. None of these three categories of elements—acts, motives, and manners of action—is by itself sufficient to account fully for the scope of moral appraisal or the needs of moral education and ethical leadership. Aiming at adequacy in relation to any one of the categories is too limited an ethical aspiration. But reflection on the three taken together goes a good distance toward accounting for the moral standards we should live by. The complexity and value of persons themselves demands of us conduct toward them that, in our deeds, our motives, and the manner of our actions, is adequate to their worth.

INDEX

supervenience 5, 94
  strong 5
  See also consequentiality.

thick moral question. *See* moral
  questions, thick and thin
thin moral question. *See* moral
  questions, thick and thin
Thomson, Judith 161 n.1
Timmermann, Jens xiii, 117 n.2,
  162 n.2
Timmons, Mark xiii, 62 n.3,
  162 n.2
treatment 2, 8, 20-21, 42-4, 56-7,
  77-8, 85, 92 n.7, 97-8, 101
  as an end. *See* treatment,
    end-regarding.
  as a mere means 24-5
  as if an end 101
  by institutions 77-8
  compound 97
  consequential
    description of 44
  end-regarding (as an end) 2,
    16-18, 26-7, 85, 101. *See also*
    good of persons.
  epistemic view of 98
  irreversible 35, 38
  instrumental (as a
    means) 2, 15-27
  merely instrumental 2, 19-26,
    30-31, 56-7

of a person 16-21
purely as an end 92 n.7
purely instrumental 15
reversibility of 30-31, 35, 38
rights-respecting 130-132
solely instrumental 15,
  21-3, 30-3
vehicle of 42
trying 43-4, 97

universalizability 151-152

virtue ethics 2, 34, 49, 61, 64,
  78, 157, 161, 163. *See also* rule
  ethics.

Wagner, Steven 6 n.2
Warner, Steven 6 n.2
weakness of will 143
Wicks, Peter xiii
Wolterstorff, Nicholas P. 131 n.16
Wood, Allen W. 68 n.6
von Wright, Georg
  Henrik 95 n.8
wrong-making, 45, 48, 61
wrongness 44-5
  prima facie 44-5, 59, 60, 67-70,
    83, 88, 101, 113, 136, 161

Xenophon 52 n.13

Zimmerman, Aaron 6 n.2

9 780190 913748